# IN THE DREAM HOUSE

Also by Carmen Maria Machado

*Her Body and Other Parties*

# IN THE DREAM HOUSE

*A Memoir*

Carmen Maria Machado

Graywolf Press

Some of the material in this book was previously published in *Catapult*, *Los Angeles Review of Books*, and *Medium*.

Excerpt from *The New Sappho* by Jim Powell. Copyright © 2007 by Jim Powell. Reproduced with permission of Oxford University Press through PLSclear.

"Ghost House" reprinted from *For Your Own Good* by Leah Horlick (Caitlin Press, 2015). Used by permission.

Lines from "Labrador" by Aimee Mann © 2012 Aimee Mann (ASCAP). Used by permission. All rights reserved.

Lines from "Voices Carry" by Aimee Mann, Michael Hausman, Joe Pesce and Robert Holmes © 1985 'Til Tunes Associates (ASCAP). Used by permission. All rights reserved.

CHOOSE YOUR OWN ADVENTURE® is a trademark of Chooseco LLC and is registered in the United States and may be registered in jurisdictions internationally. Used here with permission. All rights reserved.

This publication is made possible, in part, by the voters of Minnesota through a Minnesota State Arts Board Operating Support grant, thanks to a legislative appropriation from the arts and cultural heritage fund. Significant support has also been provided by the McKnight Foundation, the Lannan Foundation, the Amazon Literary Partnership, and other generous contributions from foundations, corporations, and individuals. To these organizations and individuals we offer our heartfelt thanks.

MINNESOTA STATE ARTS BOARD

CLEAN WATER LAND & LEGACY AMENDMENT

The events described in this book represent the recollections of the author as she experienced them. Dialogue is not intended to represent a word-for-word transcription, but it accurately reflects the author's memory and fairly reconstructs the meaning and substance of what was said.

Published by Graywolf Press
250 Third Avenue North, Suite 600
Minneapolis, Minnesota 55401

www.graywolfpress.org

Published in the United States of America
Printed in Canada

ISBN 978-1-64445-003-1

2 4 6 8 9 7 5 3 1
First Graywolf Printing, 2019

Library of Congress Control Number: 2019931350

Jacket design: Kimberly Glyder

Jacket art: Alex Eckman-Lawn

If you need this book,
it is for you

You pile up associations the way you pile up bricks. Memory itself is a form of architecture.

—Louise Bourgeois

If you are silent about your pain, they'll kill you and say you enjoyed it.

—Zora Neale Hurston

Your mind indeed is tired. Your mind so tired that it can no longer work at all. You do not think. You dream. Dream all day long. Dream everything. Dream maliciously and incessantly. Don't you know that by now?

—Patrick Hamilton, *Angel Street*

# IN THE DREAM HOUSE

## *Dream House as* Overture

I never read prologues. I find them tedious. If what the author has to say is so important, why relegate it to the paratext? What are they trying to hide?

# Dream House as Prologue

In her essay "Venus in Two Acts," on the dearth of contemporaneous African accounts of slavery, Saidiya Hartman talks about the "violence of the archive." This concept—also called "archival silence"—illustrates a difficult truth: sometimes stories are destroyed, and sometimes they are never uttered in the first place; either way something very large is irrevocably missing from our collective histories.

The word *archive*, Jacques Derrida tells us, comes from the ancient Greek ἀρχεῖον: *arkheion*, "the house of the ruler." When I first learned about this etymology, I was taken with the use of *house* (a lover of haunted house stories, I'm a sucker for architecture metaphors), but it is the power, the authority, that is the most telling element. What is placed in or left out of the archive is a political act, dictated by the archivist and the political context in which she lives. This is true whether it's a parent deciding what's worth recording of a child's early life or—like Europe and its *Stolpersteine*, its "stumbling blocks"—a continent publicly reckoning with its past. *Here is where Sebastian took his first fat-footed baby steps; here is the house where Judith was living when we took her to her death.*

Sometimes the proof is never committed to the archive—it is not considered important enough to record, or if it is, not important enough to preserve. Sometimes there is a deliberate act of destruction: consider the more explicit letters between Eleanor Roosevelt and Lorena Hickok, burned by Hickok for their lack of discretion. Almost certainly erotic and gay as hell, especially considering what wasn't burned. ("I'm getting so hungry to see you.")[1]

The late queer theorist José Esteban Muñoz pointed out that "queerness has an especially vexed relationship to evidence. . . . When the historian of queer experience attempts to document a queer past, there is often a gatekeeper, representing a straight present." What gets left behind? Gaps

---

1. Eleanor Roosevelt to Lorena Hickock, November 17, 1933.

where people never see themselves or find information about themselves. Holes that make it impossible to give oneself a context. Crevices people fall into. Impenetrable silence.

The complete archive is mythological, possible only in theory; somewhere in Jorge Luis Borges's Total Library, perhaps, buried under the detailed history of the future and his dreams and half dreams at dawn on August 14, 1934. But we can try. "How does one tell impossible stories?" Hartman asks, and she suggests many avenues: "advancing a series of speculative arguments," "exploiting the capacities of the subjunctive (a grammatical mood that expresses doubts, wishes, and possibilities)," writing history "with and against the archive," "imagining what cannot be verified."

The abused woman has certainly been around as long as human beings have been capable of psychological manipulation and interpersonal violence, but as a generally understood concept it—and she—did not exist until about fifty years ago. The conversation about domestic abuse within queer communities is even newer, and even more shadowed. As we consider the forms intimate violence takes today, each new concept—the male victim, the female perpetrator, queer abusers, and the queer abused—reveals itself as another ghost that has always been here, haunting the ruler's house. Modern academics, writers, and thinkers have new tools to delve back into the archives in the same way that historians and scholars have made their understanding of contemporary queer sexuality reverberate through the past. Consider: What is the topography of these holes? Where do the lacunae live? How do we move toward wholeness? How do we do right by the wronged people of the past without physical evidence of their suffering? How do we direct our record keeping toward justice?

The memoir is, at its core, an act of resurrection. Memoirists re-create the past, reconstruct dialogue. They summon meaning from events that have long been dormant. They braid the clays of memory and essay and fact and perception together, smash them into a ball, roll them flat. They manipulate time; resuscitate the dead. They put themselves, and others, into necessary context.

I enter into the archive that domestic abuse between partners who share a gender identity is both possible and not uncommon, and that it can look something like this. I speak into the silence. I toss the stone of my story into a vast crevice; measure the emptiness by its small sound.

# I

Eros limbslackener shakes me again—
that sweet, bitter, impossible creature.

—Sappho, as translated by Jim Powell

## *Dream House as* Not a Metaphor

I daresay you have heard of the Dream House? It is, as you know, a real place. It stands upright. It is next to a forest and at the rim of a sward. It has a foundation, though rumors of the dead buried within it are, almost certainly, a fiction. There used to be a swing dangling from a tree branch but now it's just a rope, with a single knot swaying in the wind. You may have heard stories about the landlord, but I assure you they are untrue. After all, the landlord is not a man but an entire university. A tiny city of landlords! Can you imagine?

Most of your assumptions are correct: it has floors and walls and windows and a roof. If you are assuming there are two bedrooms, you are both right and wrong. Who is to say that there are only two bedrooms? Every room can be a bedroom: you only need a bed, or not even that. You only need to sleep there. The inhabitant gives the room its purpose. Your actions are mightier than any architect's intentions.

I bring this up because it is important to remember that the Dream House is real. It is as real as the book you are holding in your hands, though significantly less terrifying. If I cared to, I could give you its address, and you could drive there in your own car and sit in front of that Dream House and try to imagine the things that have happened inside. I wouldn't recommend it. But you could. No one would stop you.

# *Dream House as* Picaresque

Before I met the woman from the Dream House, I lived in a tiny two-bedroom in Iowa City. The house was a mess: owned by a slumlord, slowly falling apart, full of eclectic, nightmarish details. There was a room in the basement—my roommates and I called it the murder room—with blood-red floors, walls, and ceiling, further improved by a secret hatch and a nonfunctional landline phone. Elsewhere in the basement, a Lovecraftian heating system reached long tentacles up into the rest of the house. When it was humid, the front door swelled in its frame and refused to open, like a punched eye. The yard was huge and pocked with a fire pit and edged with poison ivy, trees, a rotting fence.

I lived with John and Laura and their cat, Tokyo. They were a couple; long-legged and pale, erstwhile Floridians who'd gone to hippie college to-gether and had come to Iowa for their respective graduate degrees. The living embodiment of Florida camp and eccentricity, and, ultimately, the only thing that, post–Dream House, would keep the state in my good graces.

Laura looked like an old-fashioned movie star: wide-eyed and ethereal. She was dry and disdainful and wickedly funny; she wrote poetry and was pursuing a degree in library science. She *felt* like a librarian, like the wise conduit for public knowledge, as if she could lead you anywhere you needed to be. John, on the other hand, looked like a grunge rocker-cum-offbeat-professor who'd discovered God. He made kimchi and sauerkraut in huge mason jars he monitored on the kitchen counter like a mad botanist; he once spent an hour describing the plot of *Against Nature* to me in exquisite detail, including his favorite scene, in which the eccentric and vile antihero encrusts a tortoise's shell with exotic jewels and the poor creature, "unable to support the dazzling luxury imposed on it," dies from the weight. When I first met John, he said to me, "I got a tattoo, do you want to see?" And I said, "Yes," and he said, "Okay, it's gonna look like I'm showing you my junk but I'm not, I swear," and when he lifted the leg of his shorts high on his thigh there was a stick-and-poke tattoo of an upside-down church. "Is that an upside-down church?" I asked, and he smiled and wiggled his eyebrows—not lasciviously, but with genuine mischief—and said, "Upside down *according to who?*" Once, when Laura came out of their bedroom in cutoffs and a bikini top, John looked at her with real, uncomplicated love and said, "Girl, I want to dig you a watering hole."

Like a picara, I have spent my adulthood bopping from city to city, acquiring kindred spirits at every stop; a group of guardians who have taken good care of me (a tender of guardians, a dearheart of guardians). My friend Amanda from college, my roommate and housemate until I was twenty-two, whose sharp and logical mind, flat affect, and dry sense of humor witnessed my evolution from messy teenager to messy semiadult. Anne—a rugby player with dyed-pink hair, the first vegetarian and lesbian I ever met—who'd overseen my coming-out like a benevolent gay goddess. Leslie, who coached me through my first bad breakup with brie and two-dollar bottles of wine and time with her animals, including a stocky brown pit bull named Molly who would lick my face until I dissolved into hysterics. Everyone who ever read and commented on my LiveJournal, which I dutifully kept from ages fifteen to twenty-five, spilling my guts to a motley crew of poets, queer weirdos, programmers, RPG buffs, and fanfic writers.

John and Laura were like that. They were always there, intimate with each other in one way and intimate with me in another, as if I were a beloved sibling. They weren't watching over me, exactly; they were the protagonists of their own stories.

But this story? This one's mine.

# *Dream House as* Perpetual Motion Machine

There's this game I played during gym class when I was eight, when they sent me to the outfield during baseball. I would stand so far from everyone else that the balls my classmates hit could never reach me, and our gym teacher didn't seem to notice that I was sitting open-legged in the tall grass.

The teacher, Ms. Lily, was short and stocky and had a cropped haircut, and one of the kids in my class called her a lesbian. I had no idea what that meant; I'm not sure he did, either. It was 1994. Ms. Lily wore baggy athletic pants with patches of neon greens and purples in abstract, eye-searing patterns. (When I learned the story of Joseph and his coat of many colors in Sunday school, all I could think of was Ms. Lily's outfit.) The synthetic fabric hissed when she walked; you could always hear her coming. I have a clear memory of her trying to explain body isolation to us—she drew a line down the center of herself, starting at the top of her head. When she reached her crotch, kids giggled. From there, she showed us our left sides and our right sides, how to move each independently and then in tandem. She spun her arms like a carnival ride.

*Fitness!*, she'd say, touching her right hand to her left foot, then her left hand to her right foot. *You only have one body! You have to take care of it!* Maybe she *was* a lesbian.

Sitting in the grass during those baseball games, I'd rip up all of the weeds within my reach, leaving my hands smelling like dirt and wild onions. I broke dandelion stems and marveled at their sticky white milk. The game is this: You take the dandelion and rub it hard beneath your chin—in my case, right over the narrow white scar I earned falling in the tub when I was a toddler—so hard the florets begin to disintegrate. If your chin turns yellow, it means you're in love.

At eight I was reed-thin, anxious. I was too tightly wound to be dreamy, most of the time, but sitting in the grass gave me a kind of peace. Every class

I took that dandelion's severed head and worked it against my chin until it was a hot, wet ball, like a bud that hadn't yet opened.

The trick, or maybe it's the punch line, is that the yellow always comes off on your skin. The dandelion yields every time. It has no wiles, no secrets, no sense of self-preservation. And so it goes that, even as children, we understand something we cannot articulate: The diagnosis never changes. We will always be hungry, will always want. Our bodies and minds will always crave something, even if we don't recognize it.

And in the same way the dandelion's destruction tells us about ourselves, so does our own destruction: our bodies are ecosystems, and they shed and replace and repair until we die. And when we die, our bodies feed the hungry earth, our cells becoming part of other cells, and in the world of the living, where we used to be, people kiss and hold hands and fall in love and fuck and laugh and cry and hurt others and nurse broken hearts and start wars and pull sleeping children out of car seats and shout at each other. If you could harness that energy—that constant, roving hunger—you could do wonders with it. You could push the earth inch by inch through the cosmos until it collided heart-first with the sun.

# Dream House as an Exercise in Point of View

You were not always just a You. I was whole—a symbiotic relationship between my best and worst parts—and then, in one sense of the definition, I was cleaved: a neat lop that took first person—that assured, confident woman, the girl detective, the adventurer—away from second, who was always anxious and vibrating like a too-small breed of dog.

I left, and then lived: moved to the East Coast, wrote a book, moved in with a beautiful woman, got married, bought a rambling Victorian in Philadelphia. Learned things: how to make Manhattans and use starchy pasta water to create sauces and keep succulents alive.

But you. You took a job as a standardized-test grader. You drove seven hours to Indiana every other week for a year. You churned out mostly garbage for the second half of your MFA. You cried in front of many people. You missed readings, parties, the supermoon. You tried to tell your story to people who didn't know how to listen. You made a fool of yourself, in more ways than one.

I thought you died, but writing this, I'm not sure you did.

# *Dream House as* Inciting Incident

You meet her on a weeknight, at dinner with a mutual friend in a diner in Iowa City where the walls are windows. She is sweaty, having just come from the gym, her white-blonde hair pulled back in a short ponytail. She has a dazzling smile, a raspy voice that sounds like a wheelbarrow being dragged over stones. She is that mix of butch and femme that drives you crazy.

You and your friend are talking about television when she arrives; you have been complaining about men's stories, men's stories, how everything is men's stories. She laughs, agrees. She tells you she's freshly transplanted from New York, drawing unemployment insurance and applying to MFA programs. She's a writer too.

Every time she speaks, you feel something inside you drop. You will remember so little about the dinner except that, at the end of it, you want to prolong the evening and so you order tea of all things. You drink it—a mouthful of heat and herb, scorching the roof of your mouth—while trying not to stare at her, trying to be charming and nonchalant while desire gathers in your limbs. Your female crushes were always floating past you, out of reach, but she touches your arm and looks directly at you and you feel like a child buying something with her own money for the first time.

# *Dream House as* Memory Palace

From the street, here is the house. There is a front door, but you never go in the front door.

Here is what lines the driveway: all the boys who liked you as a girl. Colin, the dentist's son, who told you in a soft voice that your dress was beautiful. You looked down to confirm for yourself, and then skipped merrily away. (A diva, even then! Your mother told you this story; you were so young you did not remember it on your own.) Seth, who, in sixth grade, bought you the brand-new Animorphs book—the one where Cassie transmogrifies into a butterfly on the cover—and had his mother drive him to your house so he could give it to you. Adam, your beloved friend who worked at the local movie theater and brought home garbage bags of day-old popcorn so you could watch movies your parents would never let you see: *Memento* and *Dancer in the Dark* and *Pulp Fiction* and *Mulholland Drive* and *Y Tu Mamá También*. Adam burned you so many CDs. Some of them were too weird for you. There was one band who just destroyed instruments into microphones, and you rolled your eyes and said, "This is stupid." But then Adam's mom took both of you to Philadelphia in January to see a Godspeed You! Black Emperor concert. The band started late, and you huddled together in a shared hoodie. The music was byzantine, kaleidoscopic, inexpressibly beautiful. You didn't know how to even talk about the mix of audio and sound, the way the symphony of it washed over you, vibrated every part of your body. Once, Adam wrote a story about you and later, a song, when you went away to college. You did not know what to do with Adam's love, the steady and undemanding affection of it. Then, Tracey, who had a twin brother, Timmy. They were Mormon and sweet, and you had a crush on Timmy, but Tracey had a crush on you. You once ordered a free Book of Mormon from the internet and ended up having a two-hour-long conversation with a young guy—he sounded so handsome—who was calling from Salt Lake City to gauge your interest in their religion. You couldn't say, "I ordered it because I am in love with one half of a set of Mormon twins and the other half has a crush on me." So instead, you bantered about theology for two hours before you regretfully got off the phone. Anyway, those boys. You were suspicious of their feelings because you had no reason to love yourself—not your body, not your mind. You rejected so much gentleness. What were you looking for?

The back patio: college. So many unrequited crushes, and—ultimately—the worst sex. You once drove across four states to sleep with a man in upstate New York in the dead of winter. It was so cold your drugstore-brand astringent face wash froze in its tube. The sex was bad, obviously, but what you remember most clearly is what you *wanted* from that night. You wanted that drive-across-four-states desire. You wanted someone to be obsessed with you. How could you accomplish that? You were awake all night staring at the streetlight in the parking lot outside his bedroom window. Why did men never own curtains? How do you get someone you want to want you? Why did no one love you?

The kitchen: OkCupid, Craigslist. Living in California and trying to date women, but failing because Bay Area lesbians proved to be pretty testy about the whole bisexual thing. So then, a parade of men: sweet men and terrible men and older men. Professionals and students. An astrophysicist, several programmers. One guy with a boat in the Berkeley marina. Then, moving to Iowa and going on a bunch of terrible dates, including with a man you kept seeing later in the waiting room of your therapist's office. He played piano. A med student, maybe? You can barely remember.

The living room, the office, the bathroom: boyfriends, or something approximating them. Casey and Paul and Al. Casey was the worst. Al was the kindest. Paul was knock-you-sideways perfect; he fucked you and fed you and tried to teach you to love California. It was all you ever wanted. He was so pretty. You loved his downy ass, his surprisingly soft scruff, the strength of his hands. You wanted to crawl up inside him and have him crawl up inside you. He made you feel special and sexy and smart. He broke up with you because he didn't love you, which is a very good reason to break up with somebody, even though at the time you wanted to die.

The bedroom: don't go in there.

# *Dream House as* Time Travel

One of the questions that has haunted you: Would knowing have made you dumber or smarter? If, one day, a milky portal had opened up in your bedroom and an older version of yourself had stepped out and told you what you know now, would you have listened? You like to think so, but you'd probably be lying; you didn't listen to any of your smarter, wiser friends when they confessed they were worried about you, so why on earth would you listen to a version of yourself who wrecked her way out of a time orifice like a newborn?

There is a theory about time travel called the Novikov self-consistency principle, wherein Novikov asserts that if time travel *were* possible, it would still be impossible to travel back in time and alter events that have already taken place. If present-day you could return to the past, you could certainly make observations that felt *new*—observations that had the benefit of real-time hindsight—but you'd be unable to, say, prevent your parents from meeting, since that, by definition, had already happened. To do so, Novikov says, would be as impossible as jumping through a brick wall. Time—the plot of it—is fixed.

No, Novikov's time traveler is the tragic dupe who realizes too late her trip to the past is what sealed the very fate she'd meant to prevent. Maybe you mistook your future voice shouting through the walls for something else: a heartbeat pacing and then rapid with want, a purr.

# Dream House as a Stranger Comes to Town

One day, she texts you to ask if you can give her a ride to the Cedar Rapids airport. She needs to pick up her girlfriend, Val, who is visiting from out of town. You agree because, of course. Historically you've done just about anything for a beautiful woman. (Years ago, when you lived in California, your stunningly gorgeous coworker called you at seven in the morning because she needed help jump-starting her car. You were out of bed and on your way in ten minutes, and when you opened the hood of her car you made a point of contemplating the machinery below you, as if you had any idea what it meant.)

In the car, you are so busy talking you miss the exit—blowing past a strip club, Woody's, and the sign for the airport. When you finally arrive and park your car, you walk to the baggage claim and watch these two beautiful, tiny women run at each other. One brunette, one blonde; like Jane Russell and Marilyn Monroe. The blonde sits and the brunette crawls in her lap; they laugh and kiss. (You would love that version of *Gentlemen Prefer Blondes*.) You turn away and examine a poster for the University of Iowa very closely.

In the car, the brunette laughs easily and openly at all of your jokes. You watch her surreptitiously in the rearview mirror. You drop them off back in town.

A few days later, you're talking to your mutual friend. "I think she likes you," she says.

"She's really hot," you say. "But she's seeing someone. I just, like, literally picked up her girlfriend from the airport."

"Oh yeah," your friend says. "They're in an open relationship, though. That's what she told me. I'm just saying." She throws up her hands with mock innocence. "She's mentioned you a bunch."

Your heart launches itself against your rib cage like an animal.

# *Dream House as* Lesbian Cult Classic

You arrange to hang out at her house. You are going to watch *The Brave Little Toaster*, a movie you haven't seen since childhood but that you remember loving and being terrified of.

You sit inches from each other on a green velvet couch, drinks sweating on the coffee table. When your favorite number is on—the junkyard cars singing bleakly of their erstwhile lives, reminding you that they are now worthless and about to die—her index finger drifts against your hand, and you feel a clench of desire. You know this move. You've done this move a thousand times: I am too shy to turn to you and tell you what I want; instead, I will pretend that I am not quite in control of this single, nomadic digit. The movie ends, and you both sit there in the dark. You start to nervously chatter about trivia—"Did you know the story this movie is based on won a Nebula Award? It—"

She kisses you.

Upstairs, you both tumble onto her bed. She never kisses you in the same place twice. Then she says, "I'd like to take your shirt off. May I?" And you nod, and she does. She slides her hand around your bra clasp. "Is this all right?" she asks. The room smells like lavender, or maybe you just remember that because her comforter was lavender. Every time her hand moves somewhere else, she whispers, "May I?" and the thrill of saying yes, yes, is like the pulsing of the tide over your face, and you would gladly drown that way, giving permission.

# *Dream House as* Famous Last Words

"We can fuck," she says, "but we can't fall in love."[2]

---

2. Stith Thompson, *Motif-Index of Folk-Literature: A Classification of Narrative Elements in Folktales, Ballads, Myths, Fables, Mediaeval Romances, Exempla, Fabliaux, Jest-Books, and Local Legends* (Bloomington: Indiana University Press, 1955–1958), Type T3, Omens in love affairs.

# *Dream House as* Confession

She was short and pale and rail-thin and androgynous, with fine blonde hair about which she was inordinately vain. Blue eyes, an easy smile. You are embarrassed now to say that you were impressed by her in a very strange, old-fashioned way. Despite being from Florida, she had a distinctly upper-class, New England air. She had gone to Harvard, looked dapper in a blazer, and carried a leather-encased hip flask preppier than any accessory you've ever seen.

You have always suspected that you are shallow when it comes to desire, and there it was: all of those factors flipped your brain inside out and turned your cunt to pudding. Maybe you were always some kind of hedonist-cum-social climber-cum-cummer and you just never knew it.

Despite the fact that you were the same age, you felt like she was older than you: wiser, more experienced, worldlier. She'd worked in publishing, she'd lived abroad, she spoke fluent French. She'd lived in New York and been to launch parties for literary magazines. And, it turned out, she had a weakness for curvy-to-fat brunettes in glasses. God herself couldn't have planned it better.

## *Dream House as* Dreamboat

You love writing across from her, the two of you tapping away with verve and purpose, and occasionally peeking over the edges of your laptops at each other with goofily contorted faces. When you go out to dinner, she orders tuna sashimi and insists on placing it on your tongue. It is sturdy, labial. It melts there. She orders dirty vodka martinis and you come to love their brine. She reads your stories, marvels at the beauty of your sentences. You listen to her read an old essay about how her parents never let her eat sugary cereal. You tell her, often, how hysterically funny she is.

# *Dream House as* Luck of the Draw

Part of the problem was, as a weird fat girl, you felt lucky. She did what you'd wished a million others had done—looked past arbitrary markers of social currency and seen your brain and ferocious talent and quick wit and pugnacious approach to assholes.

When you started writing about fatness—a long time ago, in your LiveJournal—a commenter said to you that you were pretty and smart and charming, but as long as you were zaftig you'd never have your choice of lovers. You remember feeling outrage, and then processing the reality, the practicality, of what he'd said. You were so angry at the world.

You wondered, when she came along, if this was what most people got to experience in their lives: a straight line from want to satisfaction; desire manifested and satisfied in reasonable succession. This had never been the case before; it had always been fraught. How many times had you said, "If I just looked a little different, I'd be drowning in love"? Now you got to drown without needing to change a single cell. Lucky you.

## *Dream House as* Road Trip to Savannah

It was your idea to go to Georgia over spring break. You've never been to the South, not properly, and you're writing a story about Juliette Gordon Low and her house in Savannah. It's a twelve-hour drive, a sneeze. Plus, it's March, and freezing, and it's been a long winter. You want some sun. So you ask her if she'd like to come with you. She says yes. You buy new underwear at the mall.

She gets behind the wheel of your car, and you leave Iowa before the sun rises. You fall asleep almost immediately and when you wake it is snowing and she is speeding. You sit up, pick crust from the edges of your eyes. Road signs indicate that the lane is ending and she has to merge; she makes her move too late and hits a pothole at a diagonal. The tire blows.

You are somewhere outside St. Louis. She pulls over; you call AAA. They come and put on the spare, and the guy recommends a place down the road to get a new tire. You do as he suggests, and when it's done she takes the wheel again, but within a few miles back on the highway the new tire is flat too. You pull into a repair shop exclusively for eighteen-wheelers; there is something hysterical about your tiny Hyundai with all its liberal bumper stickers sitting among those behemoths. It is the early months of 2011; marriage equality is smoldering, catching fire in some states, doused with water in others. The Justice Department says it will no longer enforce the Defense of Marriage Act. Things are *happening*.

As the two of you sit there, you start crying. You are embarrassed that your car has failed you so early in your journey. She apologizes, says it was her fault, and you tell her it wasn't. "It's not a great car," you say, by way of explanation.

She laughs. "I guess this is part of the adventure. And we haven't even gotten there yet!"

The mechanic seems to notice the two of you—that is to say, he notices your unbearable levels of queerness, the proximity of your bodies, the constellation formed by those details and the bumper stickers and, maybe, he just has a sixth sense—but he doesn't say anything, for which you are grateful. He explains that the tire that was sold to you is full of huge, unpatchable holes. He'd put on a new one, but your car takes strange, specific tires in an uncommon size, and you'll have to go to a bigger city to find them. He puts the spare back on. This time, you drive. Somewhere in Illinois, you get a tire that fits.

When you pull into the parking space outside the hotel, she leans over and kisses you. She kisses your top lip, then the lower one, like each one deserves its own tender attention. She leans away and looks at you with the kind of slow, reverent consideration you'd give to a painting. She strokes the soft inside of your wrist. You feel your heart beating somewhere far away, as if it's behind glass.

"I can't believe that you've chosen me," she says.

In the room, she takes off your new underwear and buries her face between your thighs.

Savannah is warm and fragrant. The trees drip with Spanish moss, and the water in the fountains is dyed green for St. Patrick's Day. The Juliette Gordon Low house is a beautiful, rambling mansion crowded with antiques. Underneath the "Juliette Gordon Low Birthplace" sign that hangs over the entrance, she eggs you on into increasingly ridiculous poses; you are both giggling when you go inside. The ancient women staffing it, who are all wearing drag-queen lipstick and eye shadow, respond to your excited pronouncements about your love of Girl Scouting with silence.

The tour is fascinating. Juliette, you think, sounds like a big dyke. The guide describes how she was constantly dissatisfied with her home—the furniture, the gate outside—so she just took on their design and modifications herself. She learned to smith metal. Why is it that badass women who don't follow the rules always sound like lesbians to you? A psychiatrist would have a field day with that realization. (Though, in your defense, there is a portrait of her in a button-down top and with a hat like a park ranger's and looking butch as hell hanging on the wall.)

Afterward, the two of you walk through an old cemetery. She kisses you behind a mausoleum. She tries to get you to fuck her there, and you don't want to out of respect for the dead, but she is so beautiful. Then an employee shows up and you rearrange yourselves quickly and leave, laughing.

You drive to Tybee Island and order a platter of seafood—twisting open crayfish and swallowing scallops, eating nothing but the fruit of the sea. It is just mouthfuls of butter and water and salt and muscle. After the meal, you go to the beach and wade into the water. You see dolphins.

Every so often, her phone rings, and she smiles and walks some distance away to tell Val about the trip. Even as she shrinks with distance, she waves at you.

On your last day in town, a drunk man accosts you on the street. You are holding her hand when he comes up and grabs you. She shouts, "Let her go!" and does a martial arts move on his arm. He backs off in surprise, telling you to both go fuck yourselves, and staggers away.

You tremble for the better part of the next hour. As you walk back to the car, she keeps apologizing for not intervening sooner.

"Sooner than immediately?" you ask.

"I saw him coming from a mile off. I saw what he was going to do," she says. "I know this is new to you, but I've dated a lot of women. This is just par for the course. This is the risk you're taking."

The drive home is wild, almost tweaked. You cover half the country—North Carolina to Chicago—in one day like fucking maniacs. You could, you think, drive forever and ever with her at your side.

# *Dream House as* Romance Novel

A week after you get back from Savannah, you are fucking on your bed and you come and she says, "I love you." You are both sweaty; the silicone strap-on is still in your body. (When dating men, you always loved feeling a cock soften inside you afterward; now, you pant on her chest and slide off and it springs back to where it was, slick and erect but spent just the same.)

You look down at her, confusion muddled with the vibrations of orgasm,[3] and she claps her hand over her mouth. "I'm sorry," she says.

"Did you mean it?" you ask.

"I didn't mean to say it just now," she says, "but I meant it."

You are silent for a long beat. Then you say, "I love you too." It feels stupidly, sickeningly correct, and you don't understand how you didn't know until now.

"If I don't get into Iowa, I don't know what I'll do," she says. "I want to stay here with you. That's all I want."

---

3. Thompson, *Motif-Index of Folk-Literature*, Type C942.3, Weakness from seeing woman (fairy) naked.

# *Dream House as* Déjà Vu

She loves you. She sees your subtle, ineffable qualities. You are the only one for her in all the world. She trusts you. She wants to keep you safe. She wants to grow old with you. She thinks you're beautiful. She thinks you're sexy. Sometimes when you look at your phone, she has sent you something stunningly filthy, and there is a kick of want between your legs. Sometimes when you catch her looking at you, you feel like the luckiest person in the whole world.

# *Dream House as* Bildungsroman

I didn't date when most people dated. When other teenagers were figuring out what good and bad relationships looked like, I was busy being extremely weird: praying a lot, getting obsessed with sexual purity.

The summer I was thirteen I was saved around a bonfire at a Christian summer camp. I'd spent most of the weeklong session making box-stitch plastic lanyards and climbing trees, but now the counselors—barely in their twenties—fed us s'mores and encouraged us to think about everything we'd ever done wrong. A "Certificate of New Birth," printed on thin, grainy paper, was presented to me the next morning. It marks the exact moment of conversion at 10:20 p.m., well past my bedtime.

Afterward, I was an antihipster, as earnest about Jesus as I could possibly be. I walked around with a patch on my backpack that said "Ask Me Why I'm a Christian." I wore a ring that said "True Love Waits." I went to church and liked it. I believed Jesus was my savior; that he had a personal stake in my salvation, as personal as my parents' love for me.

When I was sixteen, a new associate pastor, Joel Jones, was rotated into our United Methodist parish. When he introduced himself to the church youth, I felt a kick deep in my pelvis. He was handsome, with a goatee and straight, sandy hair that jutted out over his forehead. He was a little pudgy, but only just. He had a wedding ring. And when he shook my hand, he looked directly into my eyes.

Joel was around a lot. He participated in youth group events alongside his normal church duties. He gave smart, politically progressive sermons that sowed chaos and indignation among the older congregants, which delighted me no end. Sometimes I would linger after the service was over. He always talked to me like I was an adult; he always remembered my name.

• • •

In my senior year of high school, our church connected with a Methodist congregation in Lichtenburg, South Africa, that was looking to start a youth camp for its children and teens. A group of adults—including Joel—decided to do a trial run, and they invited me to go with them.

We departed a frigid Northeast midwinter and arrived in the middle of a Southern Hemisphere summer. The camp was held on a sprawling farm outside town, a palatial property with a pool and a large white fountain and a gate running along the road. The campers, ranging from my age—seventeen—down to nine, stayed in a converted barn. I ran an arts-and-crafts elective. We built bonfires around which we sang and played guitar and made spontaneous confessions.

Boerboels—a South African breed of giant dogs that resemble mastiffs—roamed the grounds. There was a new mother with distended nipples and a loping gait, and her massive puppies, who scrambled over each other to get to our outstretched hands. The owner of the farm grew sunflowers, and in the fields their luminous heads were always turned toward the light—one morning he drove us into their midst to show us how they followed the sun's path across the sky. The land around us was so flat you could see black thunderclouds slit through with lightning in every direction; storms so distant they never arrived. I had never been so far from home.

Every night, after the campers went to bed, I would sit and talk with Joel. He spoke openly, honestly of his faith; how he struggled with his own imperfections: pride and jealousy and—his voice dropping low—lust.

"I'm supposed to be a man of God," he said one evening as mosquitoes chewed up our limbs in the darkness. "But I feel so weak. I feel like every day I fight against my instincts, and half the time my instincts win." He put his head into his hands. I reached out and touched his arm, and he didn't shrug it away. When he spoke next, I felt the vibrations of his voice in my fingers. "I'm supposed to lead all of these people and be an example, but sometimes I wonder if I'm the right person for the job. Maybe it should be someone better." I'd never heard anyone talk this way about himself. "I don't know what God wants from me," he said, finally. "As a leader, and as a man."

I wanted to cry. I considered my own lusts and shortcomings, the way my life was coming apart. My parents wouldn't stop fighting. An assault was years in my past and yet continued to interfere with my sleep, my ability to receive touch. I thought often about sex, even though it frightened me.

I was always crying, always uncertain. What, I wondered, did God want from someone like me?

One night, Joel and I took our sleeping bags outside and slept next to each other under the stars. I'd never seen a sky like that, unstained by city light. The Milky Way was stunningly clear; starmatter smeared across the black. There were new constellations here, on the bottom of the world. The planets gleamed; satellites slipped across the sky. When I woke up, there was a dung beetle pushing a small brown ball through the grass inches from my nose. I am normally terrified of insects, but at that moment, instead, I was cracked open, ready for wonder. In the beetle's determination and slow progress, I saw indescribable splendor.

When Joel woke, we walked to the pool and stared at the edge of the still and glassy water. He pulled off his shirt. He had a rectangular insulin pump attached to his abdomen; this vulnerable detail tugged on some mysterious thread inside me. He unhooked his pump, and turned to me, arms outstretched, and let me push him in. When he came up from the blue, he grabbed my ankle and pulled me in with him. We circled each other, my clothes floating weightlessly around my body. Only when I got out of the pool an hour later did I realize what I'd done: the fabric was soaked, slightly bleached, heavy as lead.

After we got back to the States, I would drive to church after school and just sit in his office for hours. He kept the door closed.

We talked. We talked about God and ethics and history and school; his marriage; the sexual assault in my freshman year that I couldn't excise from my brain. He gave me permission to swear in front of him, which I did, profusely. "Fuck that fucking fuck," I'd yell, new to profanities. "That asshole. That shitty asshole." Joel watched me meditatively from his office chair, rocking against its hinges. Once, I sat down on the floor, and he joined me there, our knees touching. "Sometimes you just need a change of perspective," he told me.

Eventually, he insisted on meeting outside work. He gave me his cell number, and when I called he met me wherever I asked him to go. I felt a strange rush of pleasure at this development. We'd moved past the default scenes and settings of ministry. He met with *parishioners* during office hours, with the door standing open. But he met with me at diners at two in the morning, and I saw his face in the reflection of darkened windows. I drove to his house and waited for him to get dressed so we could go out. If his wife wasn't home, he'd change in front of his open door as I looked and didn't look, and then we'd drive to local restaurants and he'd buy me potstickers or grilled cheese sandwiches and I'd try not to cry too loudly. Once, I fell asleep in the booth, and he waited for me to wake up.

My mother didn't like that I called Joel by his first name. "It's inappropriate," she said. "He should be 'Pastor Jones.'" What I couldn't explain to her—what I barely understood myself—was that Joel wasn't just my pastor. The boundaries that should have been up between us—minister/congregant, adult/teenager—had completely dissolved. We were friends. We were real, honest-to-goodness friends, and I did not have a lot of those.

Joel rarely mentioned my age, but when he did I could see the gulf of time between us, and I hated it. His words were a mantra that I repeated in my head. *It's going to be okay. It's not your fault. You're not a bad person. God loves you. God loves you even though you're not perfect. I love you.*

And I wanted him. On top of all of this, I wanted him. I knew he was married, but it didn't seem to matter. He told me that his wife couldn't get pregnant, and they'd stopped having sex altogether. Maybe that was what I sensed in him: something caged, unfulfilled. He radiated desire. I wanted to kiss him, I wanted him to hold me, I wanted to associate sex with something besides fear and guilt. I wanted my life to be shaken up, to go from being who I was to someone renewed.

In those months, hazy from lack of sleep and raw with anxiety, I felt like a calculator with someone's finger over the solar panel—fading in and out, threatening to shut off altogether. Joel, though, seemed to run on his own hunger. I wanted to be like that.

I wept the last time I saw him. I was going to college, but I didn't want to be so far apart. He assured me he was just a phone call away. "Plus," he said, "DC isn't that far. Maybe I can come visit."

At school, I had my first kiss, my first grope in the dark. I felt strange afterward: elated and sad and content and like an adult. When it was over, I went back to my dorm room. It was after midnight. I took my phone into the hallway so my roommate wouldn't overhear, and I called Joel. He asked me what had happened. I told him, one detail after another. He didn't refuse any of them; just listened until I was done.

"What should I do?" I asked him, the question slipping out of my mouth before I could stop it. Until that moment I'd been, secretly, excited, bolstered with the newness of a man's stubble across my face, hands that went where I wanted them to. But in Joel's silence, which carried a whiff of disapproval, I recalled the sin of it.

For the first time, he didn't seem to know what to say. Where there had always been smooth advice that felt right and good and clear, now there was reticence. Hesitation.

"Ask for forgiveness," he said, finally.

A few weeks later, Joel stopped responding to my calls.

I went about my normal routine, but his silence hovered around me. Was he angry about my hookup? Was he—jealous? I panicked. Maybe he had lost interest in me. Maybe I'd crossed some invisible line, committed some unforgivable act. I sent him a few emails, spaced at what I hoped were ordinary intervals. He didn't respond.

A few weeks later, I was sitting in my dorm room on my brown corduroy comforter, trying to decide whether to go to the dining hall, when my phone rang. I told my roommate to go ahead; I'd follow in a second.

My mother's voice was restrained, slightly chilly. "Pastor Jones has been fired from the church," she said.

"What?"

"The rumor is, he was having an affair with a parishioner," she said. "A woman he was giving marriage counseling to."

I hung up; called Joel. His phone rang and rang. I couldn't believe that he could do such a thing, and then hated myself for judging him. And as his voicemail message played, a small-girl, jealous part of me wondered—if that was what he'd really wanted—why he hadn't chosen me. I'd been there. We'd been so close. He could have done it, and I would have, happily. "Call me," I said, trying to steady my voice. "Please. I need to talk to you."

I took a train home and drove to the parish house. It was dark, but I knocked on the door anyway. When Joel didn't answer, I went home and emailed him again.

"Please," I said. "Please don't shut me out. Or if you're going to, just tell me, tell me so that I'm not dangling in this in-between place. You stood by me when my world was falling down around me. Please let me do the same for you."

He responded a few hours later. "Carmen, I'm okay but things are confusing. I have to go, the library is closing. Joel." That was the last I ever heard from him.

By the time I got around to dating people I was a little desperate, a little horny, and a lot confused. I had figured out exactly nothing. I came of age, then, in the Dream House, wisdom practically smothering me in my sleep. Everything tasted like an almost epiphany.

# *Dream House as* Folktale Taxonomy

In Hans Christian Andersen's story, the Little Mermaid has her tongue cut out of her head.[4] In "The Wild Swans," Eliza is a princess who is silent for seven years as she stitches nettle shirts for her brothers, who have been turned into the eponymous birds.[5] Then there's the Goose Girl, whose identity, title, and husband are stolen by a treacherous maid, and who cannot speak of her plight for fear of her life.[6]

The Little Mermaid suffers in other ways too. The process of growing legs is as painful as knives slicing open her tail. She dances beautifully because every time she steps, she is in agony. Still, the prince does not pick her. At the end, she considers killing him to save herself, but she chooses to die instead and is carried away by angels. (She has, through her suffering, earned a soul.)[7] But before that, the witch takes the muscle of her tongue and cuts through the tissue. If you have ever sliced a pork chop with a shitty Ikea knife, you know what it was like—that sawing, that rocking back and forth, the slick and squeaky give of the muscle, the white marbled fat.

Eliza, on the other hand, is lucky. Well, lucky-ish. Well, luckier. The nettles are stinging nettles, and she has to harvest them from graveyards. And she has to be silent the whole time: silent as she creates the shirts with her raw and blistered hands, silent as a man falls in love with her, silent as they try to burn her for being a witch. And even once she has finished her task, she faints before she can speak, and so her brothers have to speak for her.

And the Goose Girl? She survives. She straight-up survives. Yes, the false princess has her beloved talking horse killed and his decapitated head hung

---

4. Thompson, *Motif-Index of Folk-Literature*, Type S163, Mutilation: cutting (tearing) out tongue.
5. Aarne-Thompson-Uther, *Classification of Folk Tales*, Type 451, The Maiden Who Seeks Her Brothers.
6. Aarne-Thompson-Uther, *Classification of Folk Tales*, Type 533, The Repressed Bride.
7. Thompson, *Motif-Index of Folk-Literature*, Type Q172, Reward: admission to heaven.

from a gate for all to see. Yes, she has to watch someone waltz around with her identity on like a costume, afraid to say what needs to be said. But in the end, with the help of a kindly king and a goose-boy, her truth comes out. She marries her prince and rules with kindness and is happy until the end of her days.

Sometimes your tongue is removed, sometimes you still it of your own accord. Sometimes you live, sometimes you die. Sometimes you have a name, sometimes you are named for what—not who—you are. The story always looks a little different, depending on who is telling it.

There is a Quichua riddle: *El que me nombra, me rompe.* Whatever names me, breaks me. The solution, of course, is "silence." But the truth is, anyone who knows your name can break you in two.[8]

---

8. Thompson, *Motif-Index of Folk-Literature*, Type C432.1, Guessing name of supernatural creature gives power over him.

## *Dream House as* Menagerie

A line has been crossed—you've fallen in love. "I have to talk to Val," she says. "I have to tell her, I have to figure this out. We've been together for three years," she finishes, by way of explanation. And though everything has been on the up-and-up, you feel a weird stab of guilt. This is how emotions work, right? They get tangled and complicated? They take on their own life? Trying to control them is like trying to control a wild animal: no matter how much you think you've taught them, they're willful. They have minds of their own. That's the beauty of wildness.

## *Dream House as* Star-Crossed Lovers

One day, a letter arrives. She is rejected from Iowa's graduate writing program but accepted into Indiana's. She tells you this with sorrow, over the phone even though you live less than a mile apart.

You cry in the privacy of your bedroom. This was inevitable, you think. It's been great, but it's over.

A few hours later, she knocks on your door. In your bedroom, she kisses you and explains: Val is going to leave New York and come live with her in Indiana. But she wants you to come and visit, to continue dating. "Val says we can try it," she says. "I just—I think I've always been polyamorous, and it makes so much sense. I want to be with both of you. I want to make this work. Is that crazy?"

"No," you say, wiping the tears from your glasses. "I can't wait to try."

# *Dream House as* Daydream

She and Val need to go house hunting in Bloomington, and they want you to come along.

A few days before you leave Iowa, you find a vintage photograph for sale, black-and-white with three women laughing, one of them holding a baby. From the forties, maybe, but you're just guessing. You buy a frame at a thrift store and take the picture with you.

In Indiana you go from house to house together. You drive; your girlfriend is in the passenger seat; Val is in the back. The loose explanation is that they are the couple and you are the friend with wheels, but in every place you are all thinking about bedrooms. Do you need two, one for you and her, one for her and Val? What about a futon in the office? You all laugh, crowd into rooms. If the landlords have questions, they don't verbalize them. You think, *They can't even imagine it, the perfection and lushness of this arrangement.*

One house is magical—tucked into a deep pocket of trees, all wood and rustic, with more rooms than you could fill if you tried. You remember a puzzling set of indoor windows, as if the house had swallowed a second, tiny house. Another is hilariously dilapidated, and every surface of the kitchen is covered in clean, drying shot glasses; a party house with at least one curiously conscientious resident. It smells like teenage boys: sweat and scented sprays and Doritos.

During a long interval between appointments, you visit a pet store and see a tiny pile of ferrets, nestled together in their enclosure. You give them all funny voices; tell a story about the boss you had at a summer job who asked if she could show you a photo of her kids and then showed you a picture of her ferrets. By the time you're back outside in the sunlight, you're all laughing.

The last house—the most perfect—is owned by a beautiful young couple, both redheads, whose children come to the door clutching their mother's skirt while she stirs a bowl of batter. It is like a fairy tale. Chickens peck in the yard; a beautiful, lanky dog sleeps on the porch. The house is heated by a wood stove. You know the place is impractical—too far from town—but you love it so much your heart aches. It is here—standing under a canopy of trees, watching your girlfriend talk to the husband—that you first admit the fantasy to yourself: that one day the V structure of your relationship will collapse into a heap, and the three of you will be together.[9]

You put Val on a plane, and then the two of you drive back to Iowa. As farmland scrolls past you, you find yourself imagining a whole new life, a perfect intersection of hedonism and wholesomeness: canning and pickling, writing in front of a fireplace, the three of you tangled in a bed. Fighting with your kids' guidance counselor. Explaining to your children that other families may not look like yours, but that doesn't mean something is wrong. Most kids would give anything to have three moms.

You catch yourself mourning already. You look over at her. "Let's take one more road trip together," she says.

---

9. Thompson, *Motif-Index of Folk-Literature*, Type T92.1, The triangle plot and its solutions.

# *Dream House as* Erotica

In the late spring, you surprise yourself by asking her to cover your mouth as you come. She does, pressing a firm palm against your crescendoing howl, and it's as if the sound is being pushed back into your body so that it might suffuse your every molecule. When you are ebbing, and try to inhale but can't, she lets go, and you can feel the lingering tingle of unlanguage.

After this, you ask her to talk to you in a low, raspy stream while she fucks you, and she does: switching effortlessly between English and French, muttering about her cock and how it's filling you up, pushing her hand over your face and grabbing the architecture of your jaw to turn it this way and that. She shaves her cunt smooth, and it glows like the inside of a conch shell. She loves wearing a harness; you suck her off that way and she comes like it's real, bucking and lifting off the mattress.

You don't know what is more of a miracle: her body, or her love of your body. She haunts your erotic imagination. You are both perpetually wet. You fuck, it seems, everywhere: beds and tables and floors; over the phone. When you are physically next to each other, she loves to marvel over your differences: how her skin is pale as skim milk and yours, olive; how her nipples are pink and yours are brown. "Everything is darker on you," she says.

You would let her swallow you whole, if she could.

# *Dream House as* Omen

You both take jobs as standardized-test scorers at Pearson to make some extra cash. The building is low and squat, in a corporate park just outside Iowa City where the town gives way to cornfields. It reminds you of a job you had at nineteen when you were a glorified telemarketer, calling homeowners in the Lehigh Valley to convince them to replace their windows.

You sit at long tables where there is a computer at each station. You wish you could grade essays, but you spend the majority of the time evaluating the sort of long-form math problems that gave you hives as a teen, laughing out loud at cheeky kids who make drawings or jokes or write "Fuck if I know" where the answer should be. It is mind-bendingly boring, but it is income, and the two of you even make a sort of friend: a woman who sits with you at lunch, and whom you often drive home.

The hours are long, the breaks are short, and by the end of the day you are usually eating Cheetos from the vending machine and feeling bloated and pickled from the preservatives. You go to the bathroom a lot, mostly just to get your blood flowing and keep you from falling asleep.

It is on one of these trips that you hear a woman sobbing in the handicapped stall next to you. You pee—except you peed half an hour ago, so it is barely a trickle—and after you wash your hands you rap lightly on the door and ask if she's all right. She unlatches the door, hiccupping, a slender, small woman with huge, dark eyes. She says that she's having a *traumatic episode*. You ask her if she wants to go outside, and she says yes, and the two of you go and sit on a patch of grass by the entrance to the building. She tells you that she was raped, a long time ago, and she has been struggling to get someone to believe her. The two of you begin to talk—well, she talks; you mostly listen and nod.

The afternoon creeps by. You keep waiting for the boss to notice you're missing, to come out and yell at you—but they either don't know, or don't care. At a certain point, you wonder what time it is, but you are afraid to interrupt the stream of her monologue by pulling out your phone.

When you finally do, you discover two things: you've been out there for almost two hours, and your girlfriend has called and texted you half a dozen times. *Where are you, where are you, where are you*, she asks, and just as you lift the phone to your ear to call her back, the front door of the building opens and a herd of scorers begins to pour out, including her. You give the woman you've been talking to your phone number, tell her to call you if she needs anything, and then dart across the lawn.

Your girlfriend is glowering. Your new friend is running next to her, looking a little anxious and breathless, and gets to you first. "She was just worried about you," your new friend says, with such preemptive anxiety that you are taken aback. The three of you get in your car, and your girlfriend is radiating fury. You drive silently to the friend's house. When you get there, she seems almost reluctant to get out of the car, and once she's out she lingers, like there's something she wants to say. But then she goes inside. As you pull away from the curb, your girlfriend slams her hand on the dashboard as hard as she possibly can.

"Where the fuck were you?"

You explain about the woman in the bathroom, what she said to you, how you couldn't text because she was talking and you didn't want to interrupt her. You fully expect this explanation to deflate her rage—you even expect her to apologize—but somehow she gets even angrier. She continues to pound the dashboard. "You are the most inconsiderate fucking person I've ever met, and how fucking dare you just walk out of the building with no explanation like that." Every time you bring up the woman she starts yelling again. A few blocks from your house, you pull over.

"Don't talk to me like that," you say. Then, horrifyingly, you start to cry. "I had to make a decision, and I feel confident that I made the right decision."

She unbuckles her seat belt, and leans very close to your ear. "You're not allowed to write about this," she says. "Don't you ever write about this. Do you fucking understand me?"

You don't know if she means the woman or her, but you nod.

Fear makes liars of us all.[10]

---

10. Thompson, *Motif-Index of Folk-Literature*, Type C420.2, Taboo: not to speak about a certain happening.

## *Dream House as* Noir

She is not your first female crush, or your first female kiss, or even your first female lover. But she is the first woman who wants you in *that* way—desire tinged with obsession. She is the first woman who yokes herself to you with the label *girlfriend*. Who seems proud of that fact. And so when she walks into your office and tells you that *this is what it's like to date a woman*, you believe her. And why wouldn't you? You trust her, and you have no context for anything else. You have spent your whole life listening to your father talk about women's *emotions*, their *sensitivity*. He never said it in a bad way, exactly—though the implication is always there. Suddenly you find yourself wondering if you're in the middle of evidence that he's right. All these years of telling him he's full of bullshit, that he needs to decolonize his mind and lose the gender essentialism, and here you are learning that lesbian relationships are, somehow, different—more intense and beautiful but also more painful and volatile, because women are all of these things too. Maybe you really do believe that women are different. Maybe you owe your father an apology. Dames, right?

# *Dream House as* Queer Villainy

I think a lot about queer villains, the problem and pleasure and audacity of them.

I know I should have a very specific political response to them. I know, for example, I should be offended by Disney's lineup of vain, effete ne'er-do-wells (Scar, Jafar), sinister drag queens (Ursula, Cruella de Vil), and constipated, man-hating power dykes (Lady Tremaine, Maleficent). I should be furious at *Downton Abbey*'s scheming gay butler and *Girlfriend*'s controlling, lunatic lesbian, and I should be indignant about *Rebecca* and *Strangers on a Train* and *Laura* and *The Terror* and *All About Eve*, and every other classic and contemporary foppish, conniving, sissy, cruel, humorless, depraved, evil, insane homosexual on the large and small screen.

And yet, while I recognize the problem intellectually—the system of coding, the way villainy and queerness became a kind of shorthand for each other—I cannot help but love these fictional queer villains. I love them for all of their aesthetic lushness and theatrical glee, their fabulousness, their ruthlessness, their *power*. They're always by far the most interesting characters on the screen. After all, they live in a world that hates them. They've adapted; they've learned to conceal themselves. They've survived.

In Alain Guiraudie's *Stranger by the Lake*, the young protagonist, Franck, witnesses an older man, Michel, drowning his boyfriend in a lake that serves as a local cruising spot. Shortly thereafter, he begins an affair with Michel. After the boyfriend's body is found, the gay community that exists along the shore is shaken, thrown into emotional turmoil while simultaneously maintaining its collective routines. As an enterprising inspector begins to sniff around for answers, Franck finds himself lying for his new lover and trying to get closer to him.

Franck's decision to stay with the handsome, magnetic murderer is only a few notches exaggerated from a pretty relatable problem: an inability to find logical footing when you're being knocked around by waves of lust, love, loneliness. Michel does not have the campy fabulousness of so many queer villains, and is in many ways far more sinister. He is attractive, charismatic, and morally empty. We are given almost no clues about his backstory, his murderous motivations.

There is a question of representation tied up in the anguish around the queer villain; when so few gay characters appear on-screen, their disproportionate villainy is—obviously—suspect. It tells a single story, to paraphrase Chimamanda Ngozi Adichie, and creates real-life associations of evil and depravity. It is not incorrect to tell an artist that there is responsibility tangled up in whom you choose to make villains, but it is also not a simple matter.

As it turns out, queer villains become far more interesting among *other* gay characters, both within a specific project or universe and the zeitgeist at large. They become one star in a larger constellation; they are put in context. And that's pretty exciting, even liberating; by expanding representation, we give space to queers to be—as characters, as real people—human beings. They don't have to be metaphors for wickedness and depravity or icons of conformity and docility.[11] They can be *what they are*. We deserve to have our wrongdoing represented as much as our heroism, because when we refuse wrongdoing as a possibility for a group of people, we refuse their humanity. That is to say, queers—real-life ones—do not deserve representation, protection, and rights because they are morally pure or upright as a people.[12] They deserve those things because they are human beings, and that is enough.

Toward the end of *Stranger by the Lake*, the police inspector confronts Franck as he leaves the beach for the day. Franck is, literally, trapped in the beam

---

11. A cliché born of a necessary evil: the fight for rights. As with race and gender and able-bodiedness, the trope of the saintly and all-sacrificing minority is one that follows on the heels of unadulterated hatred, and is just as dangerous (though for different reasons).
12. This type of characterization was useful during the fight for marriage equality in the United States, but its shortcomings are many. It is, for example, not an accident that people have had trouble wrapping their heads around Jennifer and Sarah Hart, a white lesbian couple who starved their six black adopted children before deliberately driving themselves and their kids off a cliff in California in 2018. It is also not an accident that people struggle to conceive of queer women as capable of sexual assault or domestic abuse. (There's plenty of sexism tied up in this, too, a Lizzie Borden type of conundrum. Who is capable of committing unspeakable violence?)

of the officer's headlights, and as the conversation progresses the metaphor is sharpened even more. "Don't you find it odd we've only just found the body, and two days later everyone's back cruising like nothing happened?" the officer asks him.

Later in this scene, Franck will be visibly overcome with grief as the officer asks him to have compassion for the dead man, begs him to have a sense of self-preservation.[13] But even in his grief, he is clear-eyed. "We can't stop living," he says.

*We can't stop living.* Which means *we have to live*, which means *we are alive*, which means *we are humans and we are human*: some of us are unkind and some of us are confused and some of us sleep with the wrong people and some of us make bad decisions and some of us are murderers. And it sounds terrible but it is, in fact, freeing: the idea that *queer* does not equal good or pure or right. It is simply a state of being—one subject to politics, to its own social forces, to larger narratives, to moral complexities of every kind. So bring on the queer villains, the queer heroes, the queer sidekicks and secondary characters and protagonists and extras. They can be a complete cast unto themselves. Let them have agency, and then let them go.

---

13. There is a second, minor detail in this scene that sent me spiraling: the inspector asks Franck, "What if there's a homophobic serial killer on the loose?" The inspector does not necessarily know that the murderer is gay himself; he is guessing that the victim of a maligned demographic might have been targeted for belonging to that group. But I wondered: if a gay murderer targets only gay men, is that gay murderer himself homophobic? This question is something of a snake eating its own tail, and I cannot dig myself out.

# *Dream House as* Road Trip to Everywhere

It is July. Iowa in July is nothing but drama: wet heat, tornado warnings, thunderstorms so violent you have to pull the car over. Mosquitoes flock to you; your legs are swollen with their needs.

You plan your trip: Iowa to Boston, Boston to New York. In Boston she'll show you her old stomping grounds; in New York you'll both get to spend time with Val. Then New York to Allentown so she can meet your parents, Allentown to DC to meet your college friends, DC to northern Virginia for one of your oldest friend's wedding, and then down to Florida so you can meet her parents. The idea of the open road lights you up. You have always adored driving great distances across your country: it is the only time you ever feel any kind of patriotism.

Her parents don't want you to drive. They worry about accidents; they beg you both to fly. You come to a compromise: you will drive to DC and fly to Florida from there. They pay for your tickets.

Every step of the trip is sweet and sour. While you drive you slip your hand between her legs, jerk her off as you zip past cornfields and stopped traffic. (She is hot; you are stupid.) You fight near a rest stop in Illinois about, of all things, a Beyoncé song. ("If the lyrics were about how *men* ruled the world," she says to you, "you'd hate this song.") When she kisses you in a McDonald's parking lot in Indiana, you both look up to see a group of men—a risk of men, a murder of men—standing there watching, laughing, pointing. One man does that tongue-waggle-through-the-fingers thing, which you have never seen anyone do in real life. You fly out of there as fast as you can; you don't even buckle your seat belt until you're back on the interstate.

# Dream House as Accident

In Boston your friend Sam—who you still think of by his college nickname, Big Sam—overhears her making you cry, and acts cold and distant to her even though you just want him to pretend like he didn't hear anything.

# *Dream House as* Ambition

She takes you to Harvard's campus, which you'd never seen, and you find yourself engaging in some kind of weird retrospective fantasy. When she shows you the undergraduate dining hall, which basically looks like Hogwarts, you keep thinking to yourself: Maybe I should have gone to Harvard? Maybe I should have applied? You keep thinking back to why you applied to the colleges you did, and you remember—for the first time in years—that you chose your college list almost completely at random. You wanted to go to a city and you wanted to get out of Pennsylvania; those were the only two criteria. You wish you could accurately describe the bone-deep ache of walking on that campus, the too-late realization that you'd fucked up your whole life by not having sufficient ambition. Who are you? You are nobody. You are nothing.

She takes your arm as you walk among the buildings, as if you would have belonged there, as if you belong there, like she does.

# *Dream House as* Man vs. Nature

In New York City you visit a store that sells natural and scientific ephemera. Deer skulls in cases, petrified wood, articulated bat skeletons in bell jars, amethyst geodes as tall as a child, taxidermied mice, trilobite fossils, leather-bound birding books. There is something hypnotic about this store. You wish you could spend all day there; you wish you could spend thousands of dollars there. It reminds you of a store you used to go to as a kid—Natural Wonders, RIP—and how it always made you feel like equal parts Ellie Sattler and Lara Croft.

That night, lying next to her on a futon, you tell her about a fantasy you have:

"We have a beautiful home; the sort of home that has its own library, filled with books and the sort of things an amateur gentleman scientist would have had in his library in the nineteen-tens. And we throw a huge, lavish party, and everyone comes, and there is laughter and drinking and delicious food. I'm in a beautiful, clingy fifties swing dress, and you are in a suit and tie. At some point in the evening, when everyone is a few drinks in, you pull me into a private corner of a small room and slip your hand up my dress, murmuring into my ear what will happen when the guests have gone home. And then later, when you have kissed the last person on the cheek and locked the front door, we fumble and tumble our way toward the library, where you push me down on a lush, red divan and I unknot your tie and unbutton your shirt, and there among the bones and the books and the paintings you slide your hand up me and bite my neck and after I come I jerk you off while dead things look over us." This fantasy springs up so fully formed it feels like it's already happened in some past era, as if instead of creating it you've just plucked it out of a soup of history and consciousness.

"Yes," she says. "Yes."

# *Dream House as* Stoner Comedy

It is summer in New York, and the heat is an animal that won't climb off. You're staying in her friend's apartment in Crown Heights, and you and she and Val smoke a lot of weed. You have never been a pot person—you have, in fact, been a bit of a ninny when it comes to drugs; when you even say the word *drugs* you feel ridiculous—but you smoke because she does and she'll be annoyed if you don't. ("What, you think you're better than all this?" she says once when you decline; after that, you don't decline.) You cough and cough because you've never gotten used to smoke.

You get so high, by accident. So high that when you take the subway to Little Russia, to the beach there, you remember almost none of the trip aside from a few bright, distant fragments. Being in a drugstore and feeling like you were a sacrifice to the Minotaur. Hot sand. Her touching your back with cool lotion. (There are photos of the three of you, evidence of your presence there. You're smiling, and you look unbearably soft.)

Then, it is your birthday. There is a party. You're too high to stand up so you sit, legs splayed and head heavy, with your back against the stove. People keep coming and sitting next to you and talking, and you keep realizing, in this drifting, belated way, that they're concerned for you. You try to explain that you're fine, you're fine, you're just high, but whatever you're actually saying, people do not seem convinced.

Val visits you on the floor, brings you pieces of cheese. You stick one in your mouth, meditate on its smooth mouthfeel and nutty sweetness. You like her so much. She is so kind and open, and you respect her fortitude. Another piece, this one salty and crumbly, so pleasant in the way it comes apart. How did you get so lucky, to have all of these new people in your life? The next piece is fresh mozzarella, and as Val helps you stand you think to yourself *mozzarella is basically water cheese* and then you go to another room and fall asleep.

# *Dream House as* Meet the Parents

In the car from New York, your girlfriend is high and quiet. She reeks of weed, and is about to meet your parents for the first time. You are angrier than you've ever been with her. "We're gonna meet my parents in, like, an hour. I don't understand why you would do this."

"You've never had to meet someone's parents when you're the *first girl-friend*," she snaps. "They look at you in this *way* and it's unbearable."

You are silent.

"They won't be able to tell," she says.

"Now you can't even help me drive," you say. "I have to do this all on my own."

You inch through New York this way, the car filled with the silent, wavy heat of your respective angers.

In Allentown, your parents are very nice to her.

# *Dream House as* Here Comes the Bride

In DC, she meets your college friends, whose reactions to her range from sweet and excited to reserved. (Sam has gotten to them, you realize with a panic. You haven't successfully contained the situation.)

In Virginia, you ride horses through the woods and watch the sunrise over the Shenandoah mountains. The wedding is beautiful. At the reception, you all crowd into a photobooth. You don gloves. You hold a monocle over your eye. You cock a pipe against your lips. You drink, you dance. You love the way she bops on the dance floor, the dance of someone who has joy in her body. After the wedding you have to rip her little black dress off her body because the zipper is broken and you are both drunk and stoned and laughing.

The next day, after you say good-bye to your friends, you sit in the car in the parking lot as she talks at you—*your friends hate me, they're jealous*. An hour later you are still there, your head bent tearily against the window. The new bride walks by and notices you in your car. You see her slow down, her face crimped with puzzlement and concern. You shake your head ever so slightly, and she looks uncertain but mercifully she keeps walking so you can endure your punishment in peace. By the time you've wound out of the mountains and gotten back to a freeway, the bite of the fight has sweetened; whiskey unraveled by ice.

# *Dream House as* House in Florida

You visit her parents' house in the southernmost part of Florida. You fought the whole way down—at the Dulles airport she made you cry at a Sam Adams–branded restaurant and several strangers looked over with judgment as you pressed a napkin against your face like a consumptive—and you are relieved to be there.

She has an ancient cat who immediately tries to bite you. Her mother is birdlike, too thin, and you are worried—for her, for yourself. Her father shows up later, pours himself a generously sized cocktail. Her family is funny and mean. They are different from your family, who you feel have never appreciated your mind. And there is only her and her two parents and you are jealous; there is no other word for it.

They feed you. Chicken and Israeli couscous and cookies and kalamata olives and a bean salad with so much dill. Seafood and risotto and fresh fruit. You laugh. "Maybe we should move here," you say, and her mother smiles brightly, and for a moment you feel like a scene in a movie, a boyfriend being plied by the culinary arts of the mother of your lover. You never see her mother eat, not once.

"If you go out for a walk later," her father says, drinking his third martini, "make sure you watch out for alligators."

"Alligators?" you repeat in alarm.

"They probably wouldn't attack you," he says. The glass is, suddenly, empty. "Probably."

The next day, you get into a fight about almost nothing at all while sitting on her childhood bed. You decide to walk away, go sit in the kitchen. "I'll be reading," you say, and you do, for almost an hour. Her mother is standing at the counter, chopping something fragrant and chatting at you in a bright voice.

Your girlfriend comes into the kitchen, and asks, "What are you reading?" as her hand starts to circle your arm. "I'm—" you start to reply, and her fingers tighten.

Her mother, still chopping, says, "Are you girls still going to the beach later?" Her knife raps against the cutting board with unnerving precision.

Her grip goes hard, begins to hurt. You don't understand; you don't understand so profoundly your brain skitters, skips, backs up. You make a tiny gasp, the tiniest gasp you can. It is the first time she is touching you in a way that is not filled with love, and you don't know what to do. *This is not normal, this is not normal, this is not normal.* Your brain is scrambling for an explanation, and it hurts more and more, and everything is static. Your thoughts are accompanied by a cramp of alarm, and you are so focused on it that you miss her response.

An hour later, you are at the beach, just the two of you. "Let's go in the water," she says.

You follow her in because you don't know what else to do. The Florida ocean is like nothing you've ever experienced—warm as a bath but, paradoxically, full of threat. The ice-cold oceans of your girlhood seemed more hostile to life; anything could be lurking in this beautiful, tepid water. When you get out up to your necks, she says, "Let me hold you!"

You stare at her.

"Why are you so pissy?" she asks. "You've been like this from the moment we left the house."

"I need to talk to you," you say. "Earlier, when you grabbed my arm—that was so scary. You touched me and it wasn't with concern or love. You touched me with anger." You feel like a fucking hippie, but you don't know what other language to put to it, the panicked tattoo of your heart. "You squeezed and squeezed and—" You lift your arm out of the water, where you have begun to bruise ever so slightly. "Why did you do that?"

Her expression is flat for a half second before her chin begins to tremble. "I'm so sorry," she says. "I didn't mean it. You know I love you, right?"

The rest of the visit is uneventful, except for one night toward the end when you both come in from the pool just after sunset. You open the sliding glass door to air-conditioning and escalating voices, and as you cross the kitchen together, you see her father stepping toward her mother. He's holding a drink, and he's shouting about—something. She is tight against the counter. Your girlfriend keeps moving, without pause, but you stop for a beat and look at them. Her mother flashes you a glance, and then tilts her chin up toward her husband and says, "I need to finish dinner," before turning her back to him. The moment feels fraught, but it passes and he stalks away.

In your girlfriend's bedroom, you are shaking. Outside, the air is filled with prestorm pressure. She strips down to nothing and stands there covered in goosebumps. "I don't want to be like him," she says, "but sometimes I worry that I am." It doesn't sound like she's talking to you.

When the storm breaks, the thunder is as loud as a gun.

# *Dream House as* Bluebeard

Bluebeard's greatest lie was that there was only one rule: the newest wife could do anything she wanted—anything—as long as she didn't do that (single, arbitrary) thing; didn't stick that tiny, inconsequential key into that tiny, inconsequential lock.[14]

But we all know that was just the beginning, a test. She failed (and lived to tell the tale, as I have), but even if she'd passed, even if she'd listened, there would have been some other request, a little larger, a little stranger, and if she'd kept going—kept allowing herself to be trained, like a corset fanatic pinching her waist smaller and smaller—there'd have been a scene where Bluebeard danced around with the rotting corpses of his past wives clasped in his arms, and the newest wife would have sat there mutely, suppressing growing horror, swallowing the egg of vomit that bobbed behind her breastbone. And then later, another scene, in which he did unspeakable things to the bodies (women, they'd once been women) and she just stared dead into the middle distance, seeking some mute purgatory where she could live forever.

(Some scholars believe that Bluebeard's blue beard is a symbol of his supernatural nature; easier to accept than being brought to heel by a simple man. But isn't that the joke? He can be simple, and he doesn't have to be a man.)

Because she hadn't blinked at the key and its conditions, hadn't paused when he told her her footfalls were too heavy for his liking, hadn't protested when he fucked her while she wept, hadn't declined when he suggested she stop speaking, hadn't said a word when he left bruises on her arms, hadn't scolded him for speaking to her like she was a dog or a child, hadn't run screaming down the path from the castle into the nearest village pleading with someone to *help help help*—it made logical sense that she sat there and

---

14. Thompson, *Motif-Index of Folk-Literature*, Type C610 and C611, The one forbidden place (forbidden chamber).

watched him spinning around the body of wife Number Four, its decaying head flopping backward on a hinge of flesh.

This is how you are toughened, the newest wife reasoned. This is where the tenacity of love is practiced; its tensile strength, its durability. You are being tested and you are passing the test; sweet girl, sweet self, look how good you are; look how loyal, look how loved.

# II

The milk was so hot, she could barely let her lip touch it at first. The tiny sips spread inside her mouth and released a melange of organic flavors. The milk seemed to taste of bone and blood, of warm flesh, or hair, saltless as chalk yet alive as a growing embryo. It was hot through and through to the bottom of the cup, and Therese drank it down, as people in fairy tales drink the potion that will transform, or the unsuspecting warrior the cup that will kill.

—Patricia Highsmith, *The Price of Salt*

# *Dream House as* Heat Death of the Universe

As long as I can remember, I have been obsessed with physical and temporal limits. The beginning, the end. The first, the last. The edge. Once, when I was a kid, I stood in that wonderful sand right at the lip of the tide—the kind that could be wet and pliable or go hard like damp cornstarch—and yelled to my parents that I was standing on the line of the map. When they didn't understand, I explained that there was a line on the map between the land and the water, and I was *on it*, precisely.

Many years later I went snorkeling with my brother off the southern coast of Cuba. After dipping around the coral reefs near the shore, my brother asked our guide—a tanned, shirtless, free-diving hippie named Rollo—to take us both farther out. So we went into the open water, where if you relax your body the whole of the ocean will rock you back and forth, make you a little seasick. Rollo took us to the place where the shelf dropped off. One minute I could see the sand, and the next there was a deep, blue-black nothing. The three of us surfaced, and Rollo told me to watch him. Then he dove down and down until the darkness swallowed him up.

Even though I was safe—my back was exposed to the air and I was inches from oxygen—I gasped and lifted my face out of the water. My brother said, "What's wrong? What's wrong?" and I tried to explain but could not. A few seconds later, Rollo surfaced, grinning. "Did you see?" he asked.

A theory about the end of everything: the heat death of the universe. Entropy will take over and matter will scatter and nothing will be anymore.

# *Dream House as* Destination

You drive to Bloomington with her, because you love her and you want to deliver her safely. You don't trust those airplanes to remind her how much she is loved.

The Dream House looks just as you remember it. The pod full of her things has been delivered and sits in the yard like a shed. It occurs to you, when you open it, that someone could live in one of these, probably. A microapartment. Then you think about Narnia; the way Lucy enters the wardrobe and steps through those fur coats until she is in the snow, and there is the lamppost, and there is a whole new world frozen in a terrible winter by the White Witch.

You unload it under the watchful eyes of her parents, who observe as you lift her tiny frame high to untie the mattress from the ceiling. She tells you later that they looked starry-eyed to see you picking her up like that—like you were some strapping lad showing off your strength.

After you all go out to dinner, you fall into bed and cry and marvel, all at once.

## *Dream House as* Utopia

Bloomington: even the name is a promise. (Living, unfurling, soft in your mouth.)

# *Dream House as* Doppelgänger

When your cell phone rings in the late afternoon, you know what's happening before you pick up. You do not believe in psychic powers, but still, you are certain.

"I need to know this is real," she says when you pick up. "I need to know that you're in this for real."

"I am, I am."

"I just broke up with Val," she says. "It's just—it's just clear from what's been happening since she moved that this won't work between us. We're gonna stay friends, of course, and she adores you. But she's going to go back to the East Coast."

You email Val, feeling strange. She writes back: "I hope eventually we can be really good friends. I want to be in your lives for a long time."

Afterward, you feel happy. Then you feel guilty for feeling happy, then happy again. You've won the game. You didn't know you were playing, but you've won the game just the same.

From now on, it will just be you and the woman in the Dream House.[15] Just the two of you, together.[16]

---

15. Thompson, *Motif-Index of Folk-Literature*, Type T92.4, Girl mistakenly elopes with the wrong lover.
16. Thompson, *Motif-Index of Folk-Literature*, Type P427.7.2.1.1, Poets and fools closely allied.

# *Dream House as* High Fantasy

After that, nothing is the same. At first, it does what it is supposed to do: confirm every single sneaking suspicion you've had about your own value for so long. You are lucky to have met her. You are not some weird, desperate mess. You are wanted. Better yet, you are needed. You are a piece of someone's destiny. You are critical to a larger plan that will span many years, many kingdoms, many volumes.

# *Dream House as* Entomology

"I know we were doing the polyamory thing when I was with Val," she says. "But I don't want to share you with anyone. I love you so much. Can we agree to be monogamous?" You laugh and nod and kiss her, as if her love for you has sharpened and pinned you to a wall.

# *Dream House as* Lesbian Pulp Novel

The cover tells you what you need to know. Depraved inversion. Seduction. Lascivious butches and big-breasted seductresses. Love that dare not speak its name.

There are censors to get past, so tragedy is a foregone conclusion. It was written into the DNA of the Dream House, maybe even back when it was just a house, maybe even back when it was just Bloomington, Indiana, or just the Northwest Territory, or just the still-uncolonized Miami Nation. Or before humans existed there at all, and it was just raw, anonymous land.

You wonder if, at any point in history, some creature scuttled over what would, eons later, be the living room, and cocked its head to the side to listen to the faintest of sounds: yelling, weeping. Ghosts of a future that hadn't happened yet.

# *Dream House as* Lesson Learned

You have a redheaded aunt, your mother's closest sister. As a child you not so secretly referred to her as your "scary aunt" because she was known to fly into unpredictable rages; rages that, more often than not, centered on you.[17] You dreaded the annual trips to Wisconsin because you knew it meant close proximity to a woman who clearly really hated you and did comically little to hide it. It was a power struggle, which was weird because you had no power at all. You cannot remember a conversation with her in which you weren't tense, tiptoeing around unseen land mines.

Things that you remember sparked her anger: the time you made popcorn with your cousin and sprinkled parmesan cheese on it; the time you and your cousin tried to make watercolors out of flower petals at your grandmother's house; the time you started to describe the movie *Return to Oz* to your cousin. (It was too scary, apparently, even though the same cousin had read, and described to you in great, horrifying detail, the entire plot of *Needful Things* the night before as you clutched your stuffed dog and stared at her in the darkness.) In middle school, when you were always fighting with your mother, your aunt told you over AOL instant messenger that if your parents got divorced it'd be your fault, and she threatened to cut your father's balls off. (Years later, after your parents' toxic, miserable marriage came to an end, you traced back to that moment as the first time you felt the tiniest twinge of sympathy for your aunt, who had gone through a divorce of her own and never remarried.)

Your mother explained away her behavior with any number of facts. Your aunt was a single mom, she said, a nurse who worked very hard to support her kids. She had a disease called endometriosis and was often in pain. (Years later, when the condition bloomed in your own body, you observed that you

---

17. Thompson, *Motif-Index of Folk-Literature*, Type S72, Cruel aunt.

managed to get through the worst of it without screaming at small children, or anyone for that matter.)

Your aunt met the woman from the Dream House, once. Your cousin, her daughter, was graduating from college in a nearby midwestern town, and the two of you attended a party thrown in her honor. Your aunt was stiff and polite, your cousin utterly delighted. Later, you felt ugly with regret: Why was the only girlfriend you took to Wisconsin the one who'd reinforce all of your conservative Catholic relatives' perceptions of queer women?

After that, when your grandmother passed away, you went for a drive with your scary aunt and your mother. Your scary aunt said, apropos of nothing, "I don't believe in gay people," and from the back seat—empowered by adulthood—you said, "Well, we believe in you." Your mother said nothing at all.[18]

---

18. Thompson, *Motif-Index of Folk-Literature*, Type S12.2.2, Mother throws children into fire.

# *Dream House as* World Building

Places are never just places in a piece of writing. If they are, the author has failed. Setting is not inert. It is activated by point of view.

Later, you will you learn that a common feature of domestic abuse is "dislocation." That is to say, the victim has just moved somewhere new, or she's somewhere where she doesn't speak the language, or has been otherwise uprooted from her support network, her friends or family, her ability to communicate. She is made vulnerable by her circumstance, her isolation. Her only ally is her abuser, which is to say she has no ally at all. And so she has to struggle against an unchangeable landscape that has been hammered into existence by nothing less than time itself; a house that is too big to dismantle by hand; a situation too complex and overwhelming to master on her own. The setting does its work.

This world might as well have been an island, surrounded by impassable waters. On one side, a golf course—owned by the university, as was the house—where drunk undergrads would stagger like zombies, silhouetted on the hill. On another, a stand of trees that suggested a forest, mysterious and laced with wildlife and darkness. Nearby, houses occupied by strangers who either never heard or didn't want to get involved. Last, a road, but the sort of road that led to another road, a larger one. Unfriendly to pedestrians. Not meant to be traversed, really. Miles from the town's center.

The Dream House was never just the Dream House. It was, in turn, a convent of promise (herb garden, wine, writing across the table from each other), a den of debauchery (fucking with the windows open, waking up with mouth on mouth, the low, insistent murmur of fantasy), a haunted house (*none of this can really be happening*), a prison (*need to get out need to get out*), and, finally, a dungeon of memory. In dreams it sits behind a green door, for reasons you have never understood. The door was not green.

# *Dream House as* Set Design

The scene opens on a nondescript house in a neighborhood on the outskirts of Bloomington, Indiana, a few years after the close of the aughts. It's a suburb, but one fringed with wildness; animals move over the property as though no one occupies it at all. A front door faces the street, but this door will remain closed. The driveway leisurely loops up the left side of the property like a creek, a mailbox at its mouth. The shingles are off-white; a red chimney is the only hint of character. Behind the house is a large tree with a wooden swing dangling from a low branch. It is opposite the only door the residents will ever enter: a back door that leads into the kitchen.

The kitchen—like the rest of the house—is filled with a combination of the dense, dark wood furniture you helped her move down the stairs of her last place, and broken, mismatched pieces from the previous owner. A standing lamp with a fraying electrical cord; a small kitchen table; a creaking sofa whose springs are like peas beneath a princess's mattress. The house is functionally a circle: a kitchen that opens into the living room, which opens into a hallway from which the bedroom and bathroom protrude, which leads into an office, which loops back into the kitchen. In the bedroom: piles of clothing, stacks of books, a bright purple dildo, a bottle of men's cologne shaped like a headless torso—Jean Paul Gaultier's "Le Male"—half-empty. In the kitchen: a bamboo salt cellar for artisanal sea salt, weirdly dull knives.

Everywhere in the house, there are cardboard boxes. Not new ones, either: they are soft and smell sweet like Pizza Hut boxes damp with grease. (Like Angela Carter's Beast in "The Tiger's Bride," "The palace was dismantled, as if its owner were about to move house or had never properly moved in; The Beast had chosen to live in an uninhabited place.") It is a bizarre mix of money and trash: like the belongings of a fallen aristocratic family. There is something desperate about the house; like a ghost is trying to make itself known but can't, and so it just flops facedown into the carpet, wheezing and smelling like mold.

The curtain rises on two women sitting across from each other: CARMEN, a racially ambiguous fat woman in her midtwenties with terrible posture. She is typing away on her computer. Across from her, THE WOMAN IN THE DREAM HOUSE, white, petite, and boyish, also typing, her jaw set hard. Around them, the house inhales, exhales, inhales again.

## *Dream House as* Creature Feature

You go down into the basement exactly one time, and there are spiders down there, dozens of them. You don't know what kind, but they are big enough that you can see details on their bodies—their faces! Their spidery faces!—even in the dim light. You run back upstairs, laundry basket abandoned, and beg her to do your laundry for you. She does.

# Dream House as American Gothic

A narrative needs two things to be a gothic romance. The first, "woman plus habitation." "Horror," film theorist Mary Ann Doane writes, "which should by rights be external to domesticity, infiltrates the home." The house is not essential for domestic abuse, but hell, it helps: a private space where private dramas are enacted behind, as the cliché goes, closed doors; but also windows sealed against the sound, drawn curtains, silent phones. A house is never apolitical. It is conceived, constructed, occupied, and policed by people with power, needs, and fears. Windex is political. So is the incense you burn to hide the smell of sex, or a fight.

The second necessary element: "marrying a stranger." Strangers, feminist film theorist Diane Waldman points out, because during the 1940s—the heyday of gothic romance films like *Rebecca* and *Dragonwyck* and *Suspicion*— men were returning from war, no longer familiar to the people they'd left behind. "The rash of hasty pre-war marriages (and the subsequent all-time high divorce rate of 1946), the increase in early marriages in the 40s," Waldman writes, "and the process of wartime separation and reunion [gave the] motif of the Gothics a specific historical resonance." "The Gothic heroine," film scholar Tania Modleski says, "tries to convince herself that her suspicions are unfounded, that, since she loves him, he must be trustworthy and that she will have failed as a woman if she does not implicitly believe in him."

There is, of course, a major problem with the gothic: it is by nature heteronormative. A notable exception is Joseph Sheridan Le Fanu's *Carmilla*, with its powerful queer undertones between the innocent protagonist and the sinister, titular vampire. ("You will think me cruel, very selfish, but love is always selfish," Carmilla tells Laura. "How jealous I am you cannot know. You must come with me, loving me, to death; or else hate me and still come with me, and *hating* me through death and after.")

We were not married; she was not a dark and brooding man. It was hardly a crumbling ancestral manor; just a single-family home, built at the beginning of the Great Depression. No moors, just a golf course. But it was "woman plus habitation," and she was a stranger. That is probably the truest and most gothic part; not because of war or because we'd only met with chaperones before marriage; rather because I didn't know her, not really, until I did. She was a stranger because something essential was shielded, released in tiny bursts until it became a flood—a flood of what I realized I did not know.[19] Afterward, I would mourn her as if she'd died, because something had: someone we had created together.

---

19. Thompson, *Motif-Index of Folk-Literature*, Type T11, Falling in love with person never seen.

# *Dream House as* Idiom

I always thought the expression "safe as houses" meant that houses were safe places. It's a beautiful idea; like running home with a late-summer thunderstorm huffing down your neck. There's the house, waiting for you; a barrier from nature, from scrutiny, from other people. Standing on the other side of the glass, watching the sky playfully pummel the earth like a sibling.

But house idioms and their variants, in fact, often signify the opposite of safety and security. If something is a house of cards it is precarious, easily disrupted. If the writing is on the wall we can see the end of something long before it arrives. If we do not throw stones in glass houses, it is because the house is constructed of hypocrisy, readily shattered. All expressions of weakness, of the inevitability of failure.

"Safe as houses" is something closer to "the house always wins." Instead of a shared structure providing shelter, it means that the person in charge is secure; everyone else should be afraid.

# *Dream House as* Warning

A few months before your girlfriend became the Woman in the Dream House, a young, upper-class, petite, blonde undergrad named Lauren Spierer went missing in Bloomington. The parents of the woman in the Dream House were apoplectic; she was not an undergrad but she was young and upper class and petite and blonde and thus a potential target for whatever monster spirited Lauren off this earth.

(Years later, you learned that another girl went missing at the same time. Unlike Lauren, she did not come from a wealthy family. Her name was Crystal Grubb. The family struggled to get other people to care; eventually, they found her strangled in a cornfield. It is not an extraordinary thing to claim that some people are more valuable than others to the world.)

You were both acutely aware of Lauren's nonpresence in those first few months. Massive signs were hung and erected all over town; in them, her face was tilted, her sunglasses perched in her hair. Every time you went out, you thought about Lauren, last seen with no shoes, walking down the street on that humid June night. Where was she going? What was she walking away from?

# Dream House as Appetite

You make a mistake early on, though you don't know it at the time. You admit to her that you are constantly nursing low-grade crushes on many people in your life. Nothing acted on, just that you find many people attractive and do your best to surround yourself with smart, funny minds, and the result is a gooey, lovely space somewhere between philia and eros. You've been this way as long as you can remember. You've always found this quirk of your personality to be just that, a quirk, and she laughs and says she's charmed by it.

Over the course of your relationship, she will accuse you of fucking, or wanting to fuck, or planning to fuck, the following people: your roommate, your roommate's girlfriend, dozens of your friends, the Clarion class you haven't even met yet, a dozen of her friends, not a few of her colleagues at Indiana, her ex-girlfriend, her ex-boyfriend, your ex-boyfriends, several of your teachers, the director of your MFA program, several of your students, one of your doctors, and—in perhaps the most demented moment of this exercise—her father. Also, an untold litany of strangers: people on the subway and in coffee shops, waiters at restaurants, store clerks and grocery store cashiers and librarians and ticket takers and janitors and museumgoers and beach sleepers.

The problem is that denial sounds like confession to her, so the burden of proof is forced upon you. To show that you have not been fucking those people, you become adept at doing searches on your phone, providing evidence that you haven't been in contact with anyone. You stop talking about a promising student in one of your classes, because she becomes fixated on the idea that you have a crush on a nineteen-year-old who has just learned how to balance exposition and scene.

One day, as she rubs her fingers over your clit, and you close your eyes in pleasure, she grabs your face and twists it toward her. She gets so close to you, you can smell something sour on her breath. "Who are you thinking about," she says. It is phrased like a question but isn't. Your mouth moves, but nothing comes out, and she squeezes your jaw a little harder. "Look at me when I fuck you," she says. You pretend to come.

# *Dream House as* Inner Sanctum

I often think about how special it is for children to have their own rooms; the necessary sacredness of private space (of the body, of the mind). I am, my friends tell me, a traditional Cancer in this way: I love to nest, to make areas mine.

I had a room to myself as a kid, but my mother was always quick to point out that it wasn't *my room*, it was *her room* and I was merely permitted to occupy it. Her point, of course, was that my parents had earned everything and I was merely borrowing the space, and while this is technically true I cannot help but marvel at the singular damage of this dark idea: That my existence as a child was a kind of debt and nothing, no matter how small, was mine. That no space was truly private; anything of mine could be forfeited at someone else's whim.

Once, wanting space from my parents after a fight, I closed and locked my bedroom door. My mother made my father take the doorknob out. And while I'm sure they remember this horrifying moment very differently, all I remember is the cold sensation in my body as the doorknob—a perfect little machine that did its job with unbiased faithfulness—shifted from its home as the screws fell away. The corona of daylight as the knob listed to one side. How, when it fell, I realized that it was two pieces, such a small thing keeping my bedroom door closed.

I was lucky in that moment that the deconstruction of my door was a violation of privacy and autonomy but not a risk to my safety. When the door was opened, nothing happened. It was just a reminder: nothing, not even the four walls around my body, was mine.

# Dream House as House in Iowa

In late October, she visits you in Iowa City and decides to be a Dalek for Halloween. You are confused by this, profoundly, because she scorns the most earnest bits of nerd culture for reasons that are never precisely clear. She's never seen a single episode of *Doctor Who*. When you tell her you're going to be a Weeping Angel (you found the perfect nightgown in a Mennonite thrift store; a heavenly, draping Grecian shift in a barely there baby blue), you have to explain the villain to her. But she wants to be a Dalek, and she wants to make the costume herself; when she gets to town she begins to buy and assemble the pieces. She cuts up cardboard boxes, slices craft-store foam balls in half for the Dalek's signature texture. She buys gold spray paint. Your basement fills with fumes.

The night of Halloween, your girlfriend insists on making an elaborate dinner—tuna steaks lightly seared on each side. Butternut squash risotto. Her costume is not done—the spray paint has only just dried, the foam pieces need to be glued to the torso. When you try to gently move her along, she snaps at you, so you begin to get dressed in your own costume: the nightgown, a pair of painted wings, and white and blue makeup on your face and chest and arms. This last part takes much longer than you anticipate—is it that you underestimated the surface area of human beings in general, or your body in particular? You stand in front of the mirror swirling color onto your face as she slams things and stalks around the house, angry that her costume is not finished. Every so often, you snarl soundlessly into the mirror.

She yells questions at you every time she passes the bathroom door. Why did you insist on tuna for dinner? (You didn't.) Why did you let her be a stupid Dalek? (You don't answer.) What the fuck are you supposed to be again? (An ancient alien life force that disguises itself as the statue of a weeping angel. They send their victims back in time and feed on the potential energy of the life no longer lived in the present. A terrible undeath.)

"A what?"

"A statue," you say. "Just a statue."[20]

On your way to the party, it is an almost perfect night: a little nippy, the air smoky and sharp, the drag and slide of autumn leaves across your path. You show up so late that it's moved past fashionable and full swing, and the party has entered a scarier, darker place. You walk past a friend who has combined alcohol with something else, and when you say hi to her she looks at you with the blankest, most dead-eyed stare you've ever seen.

People keep asking who you are. You grin and place your hands in front of your eyes, the Weeping Angel's signature pose. No one gets it. "What is she?" someone asks, pointing to your girlfriend.

"A Dalek."

"What's that?"

"The most evil aliens in the entire *Doctor Who* universe. They committed genocide against the Time Lords, and the Time Lords against them. They basically destroyed each other."

You are definitely the most uncool person ever to attend this MFA program.

The woman from the Dream House, as a Dalek, can barely move through the crowd. People keep knocking into her costume.[21] You want to tell her

---

20. Thompson, *Motif-Index of Folk-Literature*, Type C961.2, Transformation to stone for breaking taboo.

21. One Halloween, when you were in middle school, you went as a stick of gum, a costume you built yourself from cardboard and tin foil and pink paint, with holes for your arms and your face. Your cheeks felt hermetically sealed in the face hole, which was a bit too small and resembled those child-sized photo boards at tourist attractions. The words ORIGINAL FLAVOR were painted vertically down your torso. It was a brilliant costume, huge and funny, but when you got on the school bus you realized you couldn't sit down in it, and were forced to kneel on the ground. All day you knelt through every class, your teachers mercifully not saying anything. At lunch, kids kept striking the back of the costume, but when you turned—laboriously—you could never tell who was doing it. During the last period, as you went to the bathroom, a teacher you'd never met stopped you in the hall. "Congratulations," she said. "You won the costume contest!" She gave you a tiny booklet of movie passes. You felt pleased, even though you hadn't realized there was a contest. It made everything worth it.

a joke—"Start yelling 'Exterminate!' People will move!"—but she wouldn't get it. You watch her down one drink, then another.

After an hour, she walks home drunk and furious. You follow her for blocks, watching her bump along ahead of you, not certain what to do because you have the keys to your house. She has a colander on her head, like a conspiracy theorist—a true tinfoil hat. You'd been angry with her before, but there is something so tender and vulnerable about a grown woman, in a disintegrating costume of a character from a show she does not watch, stumbling back to a house in drunken anger. You think, this will be a good story, one day.

A wasted undergrad happens across your path. "A ghost," he says, his eyes widening. "A ghost!"[22] He tries to touch you. You tell him to go fuck himself, dip away from his grasp, and unlike that time in Savannah, she does not rescue you.

When you get to the house, she is kicking the door. The knobs of her Dalek costume are falling off into the grass. You approach her. "I have the keys," you say, wearily. She jumps, and then begins to scream. "Why would you scare me like that? What the fuck is wrong with you?"

She is still yelling as you go inside. "Why did you want to make such a fancy dinner?" she says. "You fucked everything up, this whole night you fucked up. We just have this weekend together and you have fucked everything up." She is still yelling as you begin the laborious process of washing your face, your skin emerging in patches through the makeup. "What the fuck are you supposed to be, anyway?" She is still yelling as you stand in the shower, the temporary hair dye swirling creamily down the drain. She is still yelling as you put on your pajamas. In bed, she says, "I want to fuck," and you say, "Maybe tomorrow," and turn into your pillow. Maybe next Halloween will be better.

---

22. Thompson, *Motif-Index of Folk-Literature*, Type C462, Taboo: laughing at sight of ghosts.

## *Dream House as* Lost in Translation

How to read her coldness: She is preoccupied. She is unhappy. She is unhappy with you. You did something and now she's unhappy, and you need to find out what it is so she will stop being unhappy. You talk to her. You are clear. You think you are clear. You say what you are thinking and you say it after thinking a lot, and yet when she repeats what you've said back to you nothing makes sense. Did you say that? Really? You can't remember saying that or even thinking it, and yet she is letting you know that it was said, and you definitely meant it that way.

# *Dream House as* the River Lethe

Later that fall, she asks you to join her at the Harvard-Yale football game. It is a favorite tradition of hers, and she has flown there for the occasion, but she needs to be back in Indiana earlier than expected. "If you drive there, you can bring me back," she says. You drive from Iowa to Connecticut to meet her.

And so after a day of autumn temperatures and flask sips and people in furs and expensive bottles of champagne rolling around on the muddy ground like Budweiser cans, you sleep hard in an uncomfortable hotel bed. The next afternoon—after delays, and brunch with her friends, and more delays—you prepare to leave. She is a reckless driver—nothing has changed since that trip to Savannah—so you get behind the wheel of your car without asking.

You pull away from New Haven alternating between the radio, conversation, and silence. You scoot down through Connecticut and New York. In Pennsylvania the light drops away early, and rain glosses the pavement. Somewhere in the middle of the endless, hilly length of this state, the one you'd grown up in, she interrupts herself midsentence.

"Why won't you let me drive?" she asks. Her voice is controlled, measured, like a dog whose tail has gone rigid; nothing is happening, but something is wrong. Dread gathers between your shoulder blades.

"I'm okay driving," you say.

"You're tired," she says. "Too tired to drive."

"I'm not," you say, and you aren't.

"You're too tired, and you're going to kill us," she says. The timbre of her voice hasn't changed. "You hate me. You want me to die."

"I don't hate you," you say. "I don't want you to die."

"You hate me," she says, her voice going up half an octave with every syllable. "You're going to kill us and you don't even care, you selfish bitch."

"I—"

"You selfish bitch." She begins to pound the dashboard. "You selfish bitch, you selfish bitch, you selfish—"

You pull off at the next exit and park at a gas station. She throws open the passenger door even before the car stops moving and stalks around the parking lot like a teenage boy who is trying to cool down before he punches a wall. You sit in the driver's seat, watching her pace. The urge to cry is present, but far off, as if you're high. When she starts walking back toward the car, her eyes fixed on your face, you hastily unbuckle your seat belt and run to the passenger seat. You don't want her to leave without you, and you're not sure she won't.

Afterward, the drive is framed by the wet, dark mountains. You remember going through Pennsylvania around Christmas the year before and seeing eighteen-wheelers overturned on the side of these same roads, their engine blocks blackened by extinguished fires. And cars, too, on the highway's shoulder, casually burning. She goes eighty, ninety miles per hour, and you have to look away from the climbing needle. The shadowy shapes of deer pass in front of you through curtains of rain. I am going to die, you think. You pray for a cop to pull you over, watching the side mirror for blue and red lights that never appear. You clutch the door when she accelerates, and when the car whips weightlessly over a hill. "Stop that," she says, and goes even faster. "Sleep," she commands, but you cannot sleep.

Midnight comes.[23] You enter Ohio, a state you've always found terrifically boring to drive across, but now your adrenaline—which you are sure will run out eventually, though it hasn't yet—makes your hands tremble on your lap. You drive past dead animals by the dozens: raccoons blasted apart by speeding tires, deer whose muscular animal bodies are contorted like those of fallen dancers.

The rain slows, then stops, and you enter Indiana.

In the final stretch, when she exits the main highway and takes a two-lane country road south to Bloomington, the car begins to yawn to the left, kissing the double line, surpassing it, and then to the right, where the door

---

23. Thompson, *Motif-Index of Folk-Literature*, Type C752.1, Taboo: doing thing after sunset (nightfall).

passes within inches of a metal barrier. When you look over, the back of her skull is touching the headrest, her eyes closed. You bark her name, and the car rights itself.

"Now *you're* too tired," you say. "You're falling asleep. Please, let me do this final stretch. We're almost there." You have never been so awake.

"I'm fine," she says. "My body is my bitch. I can make it do whatever I want."

"Please, please pull over."

She curls her lip, but doesn't say anything else and doesn't stop. Every so often, the car swerves drunkenly. You pass a religious billboard that asks you if you know where you'd go after death. In full daylight, this sort of manipulative propaganda would make you roll your eyes. But now, it tugs on an old childhood fear, and you whimper and then try, too late, to swallow the sound.

When you first came to Bloomington—when you helped her find the Dream House—it was impossibly bright. It was late spring, and the trees were electric, new-growth neon green. Now the leaves burn in red and orange, and brown ones spiral away from the branches. The season is dying and you are going to die too, you are certain, this night.

The car pulls into the driveway around four in the morning and sits there in silence. You feel like you are going to throw up. The leaves drop onto the car's roof and the wind snatches them away with a papery scrape. Finally she reaches to unbuckle her seat belt, but you are watching the lawn. Two dark shapes are crossing it, like dogs, but not. Coyotes? It would have been a lovely sight at any time, but in contrast to this night's terrors it is so beautiful your face tingles.

"Look," you say softly, pointing.

She starts as if you've struck her. Then she sees what you see. You wait for her coo, for her sweetness.

"Fuck you," she says. She leans toward you and speaks directly into your ear. "You say 'look' without saying anything else, I think you're fucking pointing out someone who's going to fucking kill us. It's the middle of the night. What the fuck is wrong with you?" She kicks open the car door; the coyotes bolt for the trees. You watch her stomp through the Dream House. Her silhouette is thrown up against a series of illuminated windows—kitchen, bathroom, bedroom—and then all the lights go out.

You get out of the car and sit against the side of the house, putting your winter coat on backward like a smock. The coyotes come back, after a while, trotting casually across the lawn. Deer too, and foxes, all paying you no mind, as if you are part of the scenery, as if you aren't there at all.

You could go to bed too. Or, you could sit at the table in the kitchen and watch the scene from behind the windowpane. But that, you think, would be like putting this night in a museum—removed, too-soon forgotten. Sit with this, you think. Don't forget this is happening. Tomorrow, you will probably push this away. But here, remember.

Your butt goes numb in the grass. The lawn is a theater of wildlife. Your little car, stalwart as any stallion, sits silent and bright in the driveway, finally cooling down after her long drive. Birds titter early-morning Morse code from the trees. A gaggle of drunk students crests the hill at the edge of the golf course and stand there looking at you—perhaps believing you to be a ghost—before shuffling down onto the street. "Will we stroll dreaming of the lost America of love," Allen Ginsberg wrote, "past blue automobiles in driveways, home to our silent cottage?"

And in the same way that the wrist rotates faster when the door latch is about to release, the predawn night speeds up a little just before the day comes. And though it would not be until the next summer solstice that you'd be free from her, though you would spend the season's precipitous drop into darkness alongside her, on this morning, light seeps into the sky and you are present with your body and mind and you do not forget.

In the morning, the woman who made you ill with fear brews a pot of coffee and jokes with you and kisses you and sweetly scratches your scalp like nothing has happened. And, as though you'd slept, a new day begins again.

# *Dream House as* Spy Thriller

No one knows your secret. Everything you do (running your thumb along your jawline to search for blonde and spiny hairs, zipping up a sinewy boot, twisting a highball glass around a wet sponge, tapping a hot printer that reeks of toner, brandishing a black bottle of wine in a doorway, lift-dropping a sweaty T-shirt against your breastbone as the treadmill slows, unfolding a wallet to pay for broccoli and tissues, turning your back to a bonfire, folding your arms over your breasts in front of your classroom, writing tight lines of notes as the others talk, laughing your braying cackle that turns heads) is heightened with what you know and they—all of those ordinary citizens—do not know.

# *Dream House as* Cottage in Washington

Many years later, I wrote part of this book in a cottage on an island off the coast of Washington State. If I could choose one word to describe the island, that word would be: *wet*. Or maybe: *elemental*. Slick, meaty slugs littered the grass, the path, my porch. When I hiked to the ocean, I watched falcons dive into the water and pull up writhing fish. When I crossed a saltwater lagoon, clouds of gnats followed me as if I were the queen of the damned. At night I slept with the windows open, and I heard so many creatures: owls, frogs, and once, something that sounded like a slide whistle. Once I picked up a snail to observe it and dropped it by accident. When I picked it up again the shell was cracked, and a white foam was frothing from the site of the injury. I was horrified at the monstrosity of my mistake—the pure, unbridled thoughtlessness of it. I'd come all the way to this island to write a book about suffering, and you did something terrible to a resident of the island who'd done no harm.

One day I was chatting with a fellow writer while viewing Mount Rainier when we both heard a scream of terror. We stopped talking and stared at each other; when it happened again, we ran off into the forest, yelling the names of the others. Except for our panting, there was only silence. "Maybe it was an animal?" I said, though I doubted it.

The night before everyone had to leave, we were all gathered around a campfire when we heard it again—three howls that crescendoed into the unmistakable sound of a woman screaming. We started, and then agreed that it must have been an animal, a bobcat or something. But that didn't stifle the chill that accompanied the sound, the grievous and undeniable sound of fear.

# *Dream House as* 9 Thornton Square

Before it was a verb, *gaslight* was a noun. A lamp. Then there was a play called *Angel Street* in 1938, and then a film, *Gaslight*, in 1940, and then a second film in 1944, directed by George Cukor and featuring an iconic, disheveled, unraveling performance from Ingrid Bergman.

A woman's sanity is undercut by her conniving husband, who misplaces objects—a brooch, a painting, a letter—in an attempt to make her believe she is mad so that he ultimately can send her to an asylum. Eventually his plan is revealed: he had murdered her aunt when the woman was a child and orchestrated their whirlwind romance years later in order to return to the house to locate some missing jewels. Nightly, Gregory—played by a silky, charismatic Charles Boyer—ventures into their attic, unbeknownst to her, to search for them. The eponymous gaslights are one of the many reasons the heroine believes herself to be truly going mad—they dim as if the gas has been turned on elsewhere in the house, even when, it would seem, no one has done so.

Bergman's Paula is in a terrible, double-edged tumble: as she becomes convinced she is forgetful, fragile, then insane, her instability increases. Everything she is, is unmade by psychological violence: she is radiant, then hysterical, then utterly haunted. By the end she is a mere husk, floating around her opulent London residence like a specter. He doesn't lock her in her room or in the house. He doesn't have to. He turns her mind into a prison.

Watching the film, you feel for Paula, even though she is not real: her suffering is captured in celluloid's carbonite. You watch it over and over again in the dark: admiring the eerie shots of their respective shadows against the fanciful Victorian furniture and decor, pausing over her defeated expressions, her swooning, her dewy, trembling mouth.

Ingrid Bergman is a mountain of a woman, tall and robust, but in this movie she is worn down like a sand dune. Gregory makes her break down in public, during a concert; later, he does so in their home, with only their two maids as witnesses. No audience is too small for her debasement. "Don't humiliate me in front of the servants," Paula sobs. But even if they hadn't come in and seen what they'd seen, we would have. She might as well have said, "Don't humiliate me in front of the audience." Because either way, we—servants, viewers—are witnesses without power.

People who have never seen *Gaslight*, or who have only read secondhand descriptions of it, often say that Gregory's entire purpose—the reason he "makes the lamps flicker"—is to drive Paula mad, as though that is the sum of his desires. This is probably one of the most misunderstood aspects of the story. In fact, Gregory has an extremely comprehensible motivation for his actions—the need to search for the jewels unimpeded by Paula's presence. The flickering gas lamps are a side effect of that pursuit, and even his deliberate madness-inducing machinations are directed to this very sensible end. And yet, there is an unmistakable air of enjoyment behind his manipulation. You can plainly see the microexpressions flit across his face as he improvises, torments, schemes. He enjoys it and it serves him, and he is twice satisfied.

This is all to say, his motivations are not unexplainable. They are, in fact, aggravatingly practical—driven by greed, augmented by a desire for control, shot through with a cat's instinct for toying with its prey. A reminder, perhaps, that abusers do not need to be, and rarely are, cackling maniacs. They just need to want something, and not care how they get it.

# *Dream House as* Cycle

Cukor was known to torment his actresses to get "real" performances out of them. One biographer wrote that Cukor "seemed almost to revel in taking [Judy] Garland to the brink for scenes where she had to bare her emotions. . . . [He would remind her] of her own joyless childhood . . . and career low points, her marital failures . . . and chronic insecurity." The makeup artist from *A Star Is Born* said, "He knew how to hurt a woman, and he used it several times to get them into a mood for a crying scene." While shooting an iconic scene in which Garland's character, actress Esther Blodgett, dissolves into hysterics in front of a studio head, "Cukor had Garland so worked up beforehand that she was sick, was physically throwing up," the biographer wrote. "[But while] he might have been rough on Garland . . . it was for a purpose."

In that scene, Esther is in her dressing room between takes. She's wearing an absurd straw boater, heavy eye makeup, a cherry-red cardigan that matches her lipstick. Overly large freckles are drawn on her cheeks. Around her the room is full of reflections: crystal, mirrors, chrome; pink-and-silver cellophane around a bouquet of white flowers. When Oliver Niles asks after her husband—an alcoholic on an intense downward spiral—the cheeriness falls from her face like a person slipping into sleep. She gets up and fusses around a bit before sitting again to talk. She shakes, stammers, gasps shallowly and sharply between words, tilts her head back to catch her tears. Her eyes dart around, never settling on any one place except, occasionally, somewhere behind the camera. She sobs with abandon. Her hand goes to her mouth, as if she has just realized something she does not want to admit. She rubs her hands roughly over her cheeks, wiping away her freckles. "No matter how much you love somebody," she ends, her voice soaked in misery and resignation, "how do you live out the days?"

The scene is unnerving, devastating, wildly effective. Were it not for my moral unease about the details of its creation, it would be difficult to argue with the results: a character who, like *Gaslight*'s Paula, truly seems on the verge of an acute nervous breakdown (and, unlike *Gaslight*, with the actress not too far behind). Once they'd finished shooting and Cukor had gotten what he wanted, "gentleness and humor took over." He touched her on the shoulder and said, "Judy, Marjorie Main couldn't have done that any better."

As the scene draws to a close, Esther redraws her freckles, collects herself, and returns to the set. There, in front of so many people, she picks up right where she left off—arms flung open, and singing.

# *Dream House as* the Wrong Lesson

When MGM made the Academy Award–winning version of *Gaslight* in 1944, they didn't just remake it. They bought the rights to the 1940 film, "burned the negative and set out to destroy all existing prints." They didn't succeed, of course—the first film survived. You can still see it. But how strange, how weirdly on the nose. They didn't just want to reimagine the film; they wanted to eliminate the evidence of the first, as though it had never existed at all.

## *Dream House as* Déjà Vu

She says she loves you. She says she sees your subtle, ineffable qualities. She says you are the only one for her, in all the world. She says she trusts you. She says she wants to keep you safe. She says she wants to grow old with you. She says she thinks you're beautiful. She says she thinks you're sexy. Sometimes when you look at your phone, she has sent you something weirdly ambiguous, and there is a kick of anxiety between your lungs. Sometimes when you catch her looking at you, you feel like the most scrutinized person in the world.

# *Dream House as* Apartment in Philadelphia

Many years later, I wrote part of this book in my apartment in West Philadelphia, the one I share with my wife. Before we moved here, we'd been living in a terrible, dark building nearby. There were mice and cockroaches. We had to lay traps. One morning, I walked out of my bedroom to make coffee and found a mouse sprawled on one of the glue traps, looking like an adventurer half-melted by acid in a forbidden temple. It squealed a horrible squeal. I googled "What to do about a mouse in a glue trap" and found an article with advice. In my pajamas I walked outside with the mouse and the trap in a plastic bag, and I stomped on it as hard as I could before tossing it in the dumpster.

As for the cockroaches, they made me feel like I was on the verge of madness and transcendence, like G.H. and her passion. At first, I was fastidious, looking for a paper towel to cleanly smash them as they darted around the counter. Then one day they moved into the digital clock in our microwave, and I could see them silhouetted there. The nymphs shed their skins against the glow, left part of themselves behind. After that, I developed the sort of detached practicality I had imagined was reserved for professional assassins in movies. Then, I killed them with my bare hands.

# *Dream House as* Pathetic Fallacy

She, the woman in the Dream House, always buys too much produce. It never makes sense to you how she fills her fridge—every shelf bursting with leafy greens and robust stalks and thick roots and rotund bulbs, the bright, modern lines of the appliance utterly concealed. There is something sensual about it, almost erotic, until everything begins to go bad. Every time you open the fridge it smells more and more like a garden (dirt, rain, life), and then like a dumpster, and then, eventually, like death.

You mention it once, but then she does that thing where she repeats what you've said a few times, each time getting a little more sarcastic until you apologize, though you never know what you are apologizing for. It is her money, yes, her fridge. And her rot.

# *Dream House as* the First Thanksgiving

You arrive in Bloomington just before the holiday to learn that she has invited her entire graduate cohort over for Thanksgiving.[24] You stare at her in disbelief. "All of them?" you ask. You count the number of people in your head.

"But you have, like, two chairs," you say. "Only one small table. You haven't even really unpacked."

She does not say anything.

"You told them it's potluck style, right? They're bringing their own side dishes, and we just have to do, like, a bird or something?"

"No," she says. "No. That would be rude. We are taking care of people."

"Who is going to take care of us?" you say. "I'm broke."

"Don't be such a fucking bitch," she says.

This is how you find yourself at the Kroger's at 11 p.m., alone, picking up groceries and trying to remember how you ended up there. You pay for all of it.

Back at the house you discover that she has only a handful of pans, too, and you defrost the Cornish game hens and baste them in oil and salt and pepper, and at some point you realize you'll have to cut them in half. You're not normally squeamish about meat but you find yourself balking at the idea of cracking through those backbones, pressing glistening spatchcocks down onto the aluminum foil.

"Help me," you say.

She takes off her shirt and bra and cuts each of them with a pair of kitchen shears. The blades bite and open the birds from thigh to throat. The sound of it is terrible. It reminds you of the time you were ten feet from a lion in

---

24. Thompson, *Motif-Index of Folk-Literature*, Type C745, Taboo: entertaining strangers.

South Africa and it was tearing the skin off a zebra leg, and the caveman part of your brain was screaming *RUN RUN RUN.*

She pulls out the spines and turns the birds over; presses them into the pan like open books.

You are still cooking when people arrive, still cooking as people are laughing and eating off paper plates standing up and not quite looking at you.

# *Dream House as* Diagnosis

Should you be concerned? You feel sick to your stomach almost constantly; the slightest motion makes you nauseated.[25] There is a burning in your gut, cramping, too; acid, probably, and hopefully not cancer. You develop a tremor in your limbs, a weird closed down sensation in your esophagus. You cry for no reason. You can't come, can't look her in the eye, can't bring yourself to go to one more bar. Your back starts to hurt, and your feet, and a doctor says to you, direly, that you need to lose weight. You bawl your eyes out and miss the punch line entirely: the weight you need to lose is 105 pounds and blonde and sitting in the waiting room with an annoyed expression on her face.

---

25. Thompson, *Motif-Index of Folk-Literature*, Type C940, Sickness or weakness for breaking taboo.

# *Dream House as* I Love Lucy

There is an episode of *I Love Lucy* in which Lucy meets Charles Boyer, the actor who played the evil husband in *Gaslight*. Concerned that Lucy's passionate love for Boyer will result in some harebrained scheme and inevitable catastrophe, Ricky convinces Boyer to pretend to be someone else. Boyer agrees to play along and adopts a fictional persona, but (of course) chaos ensues, until, finally, Lucy discovers the deception.

Watching it, I can see the humor—the campiness of it, Lucy's wide eyes and mugging for the camera, the crazy plotting and slapstick chaos that defines the show's screwball pleasure. But behind all of that, he is saying *I'm not* who he is, and it is a game and she is certain but then she isn't certain. *I'm not*; it becomes a funny joke, but the joke rests on the deception.

"That's a dirty trick," she says furiously when she learns the truth. Ricky chuckles.

Even now, I feel uneasy watching episodes of TV shows about mistaken or stolen identities. The slipperiness of reality that comes along with the comedic device of misunderstanding when someone is not mistaken at all feels uncomfortable to me. When I watched this episode, I could only see the way it eerily mirrored *Gaslight*'s domestic abuse: jealousy, raised voices, commands. "This is a private matter." "You're mine, mine, all mine." All with a sheen of slapstick, of humorous distance. Isn't this funny? This is funny! It's so funny! It could be funny! One day this will be funny! Won't it?

# *Dream House as* Musical

You do not realize how much you sing until she tells you to stop singing.[26] It seems that you sing everywhere: in the shower, washing the dishes, getting dressed. You sing musicals and hymns and old songs from childhood (from church, from school, from Girl Scouts). You make up songs, too, with lyrics for whatever is happening at the time. She sings along to music in the car, but only when the music is playing. You ask her to sing to you, without music, but she refuses.

During a rare moment of clarity, you tell her, sassily, that if she can't accept your singing, she can't accept you. It is supposed to be a joke, sort of, but it lands flat. "Maybe," she says, her voice cold down to the pith.

---

26. Thompson, *Motif-Index of Folk-Literature*, Type C481, Taboo: singing.

# *Dream House as* Cautionary Tale

One weekday, when you drive back from the Dream House, you notice you're low on gas as you blow past the Illinois-Iowa border. Your GPS tells you there is a gas station off a lonely, wind-strewn exit, and as soon as you get off you sense the mistake. It looks like a long country road; just cornfields punctuated with barns and houses. You keep driving; surely a gas station will creep up over the horizon? But every time you crest a hill, you just see more country roads. Should you turn back? Perhaps a station is just around the next turn? Twilight falls away, and suddenly the landscape flattens and is swallowed by darkness.

You pull the car over and consult your phone, but there is no signal. You sit there, breathing deeply. What would your dad say? What would anyone have done in this situation before cell phones? Should you walk? Should you go to someone's front door? You just want to be home.

You have been screaming for a whole minute before you become fully aware of it. You are pounding the steering wheel—your poor car, she has never done anything except your bidding—and howling, "Fuck, fuck, fuck." You don't know why you are crying. Everyone gets lost.

## *Dream House as* Rapture

As a kid, you read those Left Behind books, and even watched the wooden, incoherent movie with Kirk Cameron. Cheap thrillers with apocalyptic themes and biblical righteousness: Could there have been anything else so perfectly constructed for your teenage self?

You were obsessed with the idea of the Rapture, even though your family never went to that sort of church. You found it intoxicating, disciplined. He could come at any moment. He could come and take the believers and leave with them, and you'd have to be ready. You had to be trembling, prepared, on edge, ready for the moment. You could never relax, never let down your guard. Because if he came and you failed the test—and Jesus would know the innermost chambers of your heart, you could not lie to him—you would be left behind, and you would remain with the nonbelievers (clutching the folded clothes of their taken loved ones) as the apocalypse tore the world apart.

Then one day you learned that rapture could also mean "blissful happiness," and you understood, fully: that it is important to live in unyielding fear with a smile on your face.

# *Dream House as* a Lesson in the Subjunctive

Yes, there are spiders in the basement, and yes, the floors are so uneven you can feel them pushing your right leg up against your torso if you run too quickly from room to room, and yes she's never unpacked and is using tall cardboard boxes filled with bric-a-brac as furniture, and yes the couch is so old you can feel the springs in your back, and yes she wants to grow pot in the basement, and yes every room has bad memories, but sure, the two of you could raise children here.

# *Dream House as* Fantasy

Fantasy is, I think, the defining cliché of female queerness. No wonder we joke about U-Hauls on the second date. To find desire, love, everyday joy without men's accompanying bullshit is a pretty decent working definition of paradise.

The literature of queer domestic abuse is lousy with references to this[27] punctured[28] dream,[29] which proves to be as much a violation as a black eye, a sprained wrist. Even the enduring symbol of queerness—the rainbow—is a promise not to repeat an act of supreme violence by a capricious and rageful god: *I won't flood the whole world again. It was a one-time thing, I swear. Do you trust me?* (And, later, a threat: the next time, motherfuckers, it'll be fire.) Acknowledging the insufficiency of this idealism is nearly as painful as acknowledging that we're the same as straight folks in this regard: we're in the muck like everyone else. All of this fantasy is an act of supreme optimism, or, if you're feeling less charitable, arrogance.

Maybe this will change someday. Maybe, when queerness is so normal and accepted that finding it will feel less like entering paradise and more like the claiming of your own body: imperfect, but yours.

---

27. "I go to sleep at night in the arms of my lover dreaming of lesbian paradise. What a nightmare, then, to open my eyes to the reality of lesbian battering. It feels like a nightmare trying to talk about it, like a fog that tightens the chest and closes the throat. . . . We are so good at celebrating our love. It is so hard for us to hear that some lesbians live, not in paradise, but in a hell of fear and violence" (Lisa Shapiro, commentary in *Off Our Backs*, 1991).

28. "What will it do to our utopian dyke dreams to admit the existence of this violence?" (Amy Edgington, from an account of the first Lesbian Battering Conference held in Little Rock, AR, in 1988).

29. From a review of *Behind the Curtains*, a 1987 play about lesbian abuse: "By writing the play [and] by portraying both joy and pain in our lives, [Margaret Nash rejects the] almost reflex assumption that lesbians have surpassed the society from which we were born and, having come out, now exist in some mystical utopia" (Tracey MacDonald, *Off Our Backs*, 1987).

# *Dream House as* Inventory

She makes you tell her what is wrong with you. This is a favorite activity; even better than her telling you what is wrong with you. Years later, it's a habit that's hard to break.

You can be an incorrigible snob. You value intelligence and wit over other, more admirable qualities. You hate it when people say stupid things. You have an ego: you believe you are good at what you do. You're neurotic and anxious and self-centered. You get impatient when people don't understand things as quickly as you do. You've definitely done some dumb things because of horniness—embarrassing things. You've degraded yourself in front of more than one person. You secretly want to be a man, not because of any doubts about your gender identity, but because you want people to take you more seriously. You love squeezing zits. You'd rather have an orgasm than do most things. Occasionally—and often without warning—your ability to give a fuck drops to exactly zero, and you become useless to anyone who needs you. You've had sexual fantasies about the majority of your friends. You wish someone would call you a genius. You've cheated at board games. You once went to an emergency doctor's appointment on Christmas Day because you thought you had herpes, but it was just a zit. As a child, you were a tattletale, and you remain an unflinching rule follower. You're a prude about drugs. You're a hypochondriac. The only way you can focus during prolonged meditation is thinking about an orgy. You love a good fight.

# *Dream House as* Tragedy of the Commons

She is always trying to win.

You want to say to her: We cannot advance together if you are like this. Love cannot be won or lost; a relationship doesn't have a scoring system. We are partners, paired against the world. We cannot succeed if we are at odds with each other.

Instead you say: Why don't you understand? Don't you understand? You do understand? Then what don't I understand?

# Dream House as Epiphany

Most types of domestic abuse are completely legal.

## *Dream House as* Legacy

She goes on a ski trip to Colorado with her parents, and you are not invited. She calls you from the lodge while you are at home, writing.

"I'm taking a hot bath," she says. "Drinking a gin and tonic. Thinking about you. I'm going to get myself off. I miss you."

"I miss you too," you say.

"Do you want to get off with me?" she asks. The idea is tempting—your cunt clenches and relaxes, a reflex—but your roommates are in the kitchen, feet from your door, and you don't trust yourself to be quiet.

"I don't know if I can, right now."

"You know," she says, her voice leaking through the receiver like gas, "if you're not turned on by me, you can say so."

"I'm not—what?"

"If you don't find me attractive, maybe we shouldn't be together at all."

You are sitting up straight now. "Are you breaking up with me?"

"I'm saying that it's really hard to be with someone who isn't into you, and I don't think I should be."

"You are breaking up with me." You feel a sudden ballooning in your chest, somewhere between panic and elation. You hang up the phone. She calls back immediately, and you reject the call. Again, and again. You start sobbing, and John comes in. He asks you what's going on.

"I think she just broke up with me," you say.

The phone keeps chirping. John gently pries it out of your hand. "Why don't we turn this off?" he says. You try to turn it off but you are having trouble remembering how, so you open up the back and remove the battery. The whole thing goes black, mercifully silent. You are sobbing in disbelief, your body aching from the whiplash turn of the conversation. He hugs you tightly, and you sit there together.

• • •

After an hour, you put the battery back in the phone. Almost immediately, it rings. You pick up. She is weeping.

"Why weren't you answering my calls?" she sobs.

"You just broke up with me," you say.

"I didn't break up with you!" she howls, and then from the background you hear her father's voice, enraged. "Is that that *fucking bitch*? Get off the goddamned phone—"

And then she starts screaming at him to go away, and the phone goes dead.

John stares at you but doesn't say anything.

You will eventually lose track of the number of times she breaks up with you like this.

## *Dream House as* Word Problem

Okay, so, there's this woman, and she lives in Iowa City, and then she moves to Bloomington, Indiana, 408 miles away. And her girlfriend, who loves her very much, agrees to do the whole long-distance thing. She doesn't even pause, it's what she would call a no-brainer. (The pun is lost on her, in the moment.) She spends the entire second year of her graduate school experience shuttling back and forth to Bloomington. She does it gladly. In one trip, she can listen to 75 percent of an audiobook. If she is driving at sixty-five miles per hour, and the average length of an audiobook is ten hours, how many months will it take for her to realize she has wasted half of her MFA program driving to her girlfriend's house to be yelled at for five days? How many months will it take her to come to terms with the fact that she functionally did this to herself?

# III

And because you are of a kind, the house knows
you. When you cry out,
the lights flicker, ghostly blue and ragged.
When she says you are *shut off,*
the light switches nod their white tiny
heads. Tiles creak *yes* beneath her
edicts—*something bad must have happened*
*to make you this way,* the way
where you don't want her. But the windows
rattle, disagree. In their honeyed,
blindless light, they see it—something bad
is *happening.*

—Leah Horlick, "Ghost House"

# *Dream House as* Man vs. Self

Your mother once owned a tiny, trembling schnoodle named Greta, whom she rescued when you were in college. Greta was rotund and gray and the most neurotic dog you'd ever met, prone to fits of ennui and anxiety. When Gibby, your family's cockapoo, died from choking on a plastic bag, Greta mourned by moving elaborate piles of stuffed animals—some of them bigger than she was—around the house. "She just keeps doing that," your mother said mildly when you asked her about the behavior.

You once dogsat Greta when your mother was out of town and you were profoundly unnerved by her malaise; she spent most of the day lying in a particular spot on top of the couch, her face flattened into the fabric—except she wasn't sleeping: her dark eyes were open and fixed on nothing. She looked dead. Every time you moved her, she dangled limply, not extending her feet when you put her on the ground. When you took her outside to use the bathroom, she went to the closest spot, keeping her eyes on you the whole time, and peed with more lassitude than you experienced in the entirety of your teenage years. When you were out walking her on a leash she would lie on the ground and refuse to move, and more than once you had to carry her home.

One day, you picked her up, put her by the door, and opened it. "Greta," you said, "go on! Be free! Run!" She just looked at you with the saddest, most mournful expression.

She could have run. The door was open. But it was as if she didn't even know what she was looking at.

# *Dream House as* Modern Art

That winter you go to the Brooklyn Museum, to an exhibition called *Hide/ Seek*. You're in duress, in the city against your will. You did not want to go to New York, even for a few days, but she insisted. You agree to go to the museum because art has always had a balancing effect on your mind; it is a reminder that you are more than a body and its accompanying grief.

Inside, you wander ahead of her, far ahead so you don't have to feel her presence weighing on you like a pillow on the face. You find *Untitled (Portrait of Ross in L.A.)* by Félix González-Torres, a Cuban American artist. When you first see the installation—a pile of candy wrapped in multi-colored cellophane, tucked in a corner—you almost laugh. It is so strangely out of place in this space. But when you get closer and read the description, you understand: it is the weight of the artist's late lover as he began to die of AIDS. Viewers should take a piece of candy, the description says, and at some point it will be replenished. Someone has been replenishing the lost ones since 1991.

In 1991 you were five. You didn't know you were queer. You were living in a Pennsylvania suburb and you didn't know what AIDS was. You were muttering stories to yourself. You were resentful of your little brother and had newly welcomed a baby sister, of whom you were also resentful. You were so afraid of balloons you invented a device made of a soda bottle and straw that would keep the latex bladder from being sucked into your lungs. You were all mind; anxiety was your lifeblood, your fuel. You were young. You didn't know your mind could be a boon and a prison both; that someone could take its power and turn it against you.

In the new days of 2012, as you stand in front of the pile of candy you feel a direct line to its hopelessness, rage, grief. You read the placard. "An act of communion." You pick up one, spin the sweet from its wrapper, and put it in your mouth.

At that moment, she appears next to you.

"What are you doing?" she hisses.

You gesture to the sign, the explanation. She doesn't look. She gets so close to you it's like she's going to kiss your ear, except she's berating you under her breath, a steady stream of rage and profanity that would be indistinguishable from sweet nothings to a nearby stranger. You can't look at her. You can't look away from Ross, who is also Untitled, who is also dead, who will also always be alive, immortal. You suck and suck and suck on the candy, which you're realizing has no identifiable flavor beyond its sugar, and she's still telling you you're the worst, you're worse than the worst, she can't believe she brought you here. (This exhibit? This museum? This city? Her bed? You'll never know.) The candy goes from pebble to ice chip, and then it's gone—one more step toward Ross's disintegration. One more step toward resurrection.

# *Dream House as* Second Chances

One day you are both napping off a hangover in the Dream House when she turns to you, wide awake—more wide awake than you thought she was.

"What would you say if I told you I wanted to apply to Iowa again?" she asks. "So I can move back, be with you."

It is hard to identify the sensation in your chest, the simultaneous leap of excitement yanked back by a leash of panic. You smile, quickly, but she has seen something in your face, and hers collapses with displeasure.

"What, you don't think I'm good enough? Or you don't want me there?"

"No, I just—you spent all of this time and money getting to Bloomington, and you love it here. And you love your friends—why would you leave? This is such a great program. I think we're making the long-distance thing work, don't you?"

She pushes herself up off the bed and walks away. She doesn't talk to you for the rest of the day. Not until you muster up all your sweetness and agree to help her. "I can't wait for you to be there with me," you tell her. You don't question her logic again.

But you know. You know that, somewhere deep down, it isn't about you at all.

You help her edit her stories for her application. One of them is about a man who is so possessive and jealous he wrecks all of his relationships. It's pretty good.

# *Dream House as* Chekhov's Gun

You'd been staying at the Dream House for weeks over Christmas break, carless, careless. You shouldn't have been so stupid; the warnings were already there, but the prospect of endless days of fucking for hours in a lavender bed and eating decadently and being with her was too tantalizing. You have always been a hedonist, and she is there to indulge with you, with an animal hunger that matches your own.

In the final week, you go to the local bowling alley with her and her writer friends. You'd driven there in her car—a sleek, luxury thing gifted by her parents—and she was supposed to be the designated driver, for once. So you'd been drinking freely of the pitchers of pale beer, the sort you don't drink, except you never get the chance to get drunk around her anymore and you're eager for that looseness in your limbs. She has a single beer, sips it slowly, smiles at you. You bowl the way you always bowl; your turns generally ending with no pins down at all, because you get too excited and the gutter slurps up the ball. But then every so often, a strike; so beautiful and devastating a crash that you get the sensation of being good at something, a sliver of confidence. You turn the ball in your hand, pearlescent and peach, and whip it down with that beautiful *thunk-whirr.*

She sits there, looking butch, and pats her lap. You sit. You haven't had many boyfriends or girlfriends, and none of them—and certainly no flirtatious people in your past—have ever gestured to you like this. You feel calm, content, a little high. Just a girl sitting on her girl's lap.

Her hands are running up your breasts before you can do anything about it. You clasp them in your own and push them down gently. She puts them up again. When you move them a second time, you can feel her anger; you can't see her but the smell of her changes, like a cheap dish towel left on a live electric burner. She snaps around you like a Venus flytrap, pinning your arms against your torso.

She leans in to your ear. What are you doing, she says. It doesn't sound like words, like a question; it sounds like a purr.

"Don't," you say.

She tightens her grip on your arms. "I fucking hate you," she says. She sounds, suddenly, drunk, even though you've been watching her and you know she's had only the one beer. But you've had beer, too, and you don't know what to do. "I fucking hate you," she says again. The sounds of the bowling alley are coming from very far away; you feel like your heart is going to stop. You are not a parent; no one has ever told you that they hated you.

You stand up and look around wildly at the others, who are studiously looking elsewhere. "I think we need to go," you say. "I think—"

But when she stands, she does look drunk. How will you get home? You reach for your wallet, but you have no cash, and after a few minutes one of the poets comes up to you. "I'm so sorry," he says a few times, his speech slurred, though sorry for what he does not specify—but then he presses a twenty-dollar bill into your hand for a cab. You tell him you'll pay him back, but now that you think about it, you never did.

When the cab pulls away from the bowling alley, you see her car gleaming in the parking lot and pray that it doesn't get towed before morning. In the back of the cab, she closes her eyes, begins to mutter a monologue that lasts for the entire drive home. *You fucking cunt I fucking hate you goddamn you Carmen fuck you fuck your mother fuck everything you cunt you goddamn fucking slut fuck you . . .*

The sensation of pulling a sheet from the bed is terrible. You will sleep on the couch. That's what people do, when they're mad at the person who would otherwise sleep next to them. You've never done it but you have heard of it happening. You've seen it in movies. You can't find your pajamas. You go out to the living room, strip down to your underwear, and curl up on the broken couch with the springs pressing into your side. You pull the sheet around you. It's that soft, wonderfully stretchy jersey fabric, the same type you had in college.

She peels the sheet away from your body; you shiver.[30] "What are you

---

30. Thompson, *Motif-Index of Folk-Literature*, Type E279.3, Ghost pulls bedclothing from sleeper.

doing?" she asks, standing over you. You don't say anything. Then, when she doesn't move, you tell her, "I'm angry, and I'd like to sleep alone, please."

She kneels at the side of the couch like a supplicant with an offering. You think maybe she is going to try to kiss you, or maybe fuck you, though you won't let her, though you won't let her you won't let her you won't—

She leans over and begins to scream directly in your ear, like she's pouring acid out of her mouth and into you. You try to scramble away, but she is pushing on your body, howling like a wounded bear, like an ancient god. (An ancient bear; a wounded god.)

It is as if something has been cut loose. You roll off the couch, stand, and dart to the other side of the room. She vanishes into her bedroom and comes out again with your suitcase. With a tremendous yell, she hurls it across the room, where it crashes into the wall. She reaches down and grabs something—your very fancy ModCloth boot, the first pair of shoes you've ever spent that much money on—and throws it at you. It spins, misses. She throws the other one, and it also misses you but takes a framed picture off the wall, and later you will try to figure out if she never landed a throw because you were so quick to dodge them or because she couldn't aim for shit, but you will never come to any conclusion.

She reaches down to grab something else, and you find yourself delving into deep wells of childhood experience: playfully outrunning your little brother, who is determined to put something gross in your hair. The house is a circle, so you run away from her, toward the kitchen, and she follows you, like your brother would when he was seven, and you dart through the office and the hallway and then into the bathroom. You slam the door and lock it, and a millisecond later you jerk away from the knob when the whole door shakes, as if she's hurled herself against it. She is still screaming. You back away toward the far wall and slide to the floor. It sounds like she is trying to break the door down.

You are there for some time, but you don't have your phone and can't say how long, exactly. Eventually, the sounds stop. It is eerily silent. You stand and unlock the door. You come out trembling, crying. She is sitting on the couch, staring into nothingness like a doll. She turns and looks at you, her face slack.

"What's wrong?" she says. "Why do you look so upset?"

On that night, the gun is set upon the mantlepiece. The metaphorical gun, of course. If there were a literal gun, you'd probably be dead.

# *Dream House as* Sniffs from the Ink of Women

Norman Mailer once said, "The sniffs I get from the ink of women are always," among other things, "too dykily psychotic." In other words, one woman writing is mad and a woman-who-loves-women writing is mad squared. Hysteria and inversion, compounded like interest; an eternally growing debt. Mailer's use of the adverb *dykily* suggests that, for him, disinterest in his dick must be a species of psychosis.

Narratives about mental health and lesbians always smack of homophobia. I remember watching *Girlfriend* in college—a rare Bollywood film about queer women—in which a wrench-wielding, butch lesbian seduces a gorgeous femme, but eventually the femme pulls away and falls in love with a dude and the butch goes ballistic, becoming possessive and violent before dying in a fall from a window.

I came of age in a culture where gay marriage went from comic impossibility to foregone conclusion to law of the land. I haven't been closeted in almost a decade. Even so I am unaccountably haunted by the specter of the lunatic lesbian. I did not want my lover to be dogged by mental illness or a personality disorder or rage issues. I did not want her to act with unflagging irrationality. I didn't want her to be jealous or cruel. Years later, if I could say anything to her, I'd say, "For fuck's sake, stop making us look bad."

# *Dream House as* Haunted Mansion

What does it mean for something to be haunted, exactly? You know the formula instinctually: a place is steeped in tragedy. Death, at the very least, but so many terrible things can precede death, and it stands to reason that some of them might accomplish something similar. You spend so much time trembling between the walls of the Dream House, obsessively attuned to the position of her body relative to yours, not sleeping properly, listening for the sound of her footsteps, the way disdain creeps into her voice, staring dead-eyed in disbelief at things you never thought you'd see in your lifetime.

What else does it mean? It means that metaphors abound; that space exists in four dimensions; that if you return somewhere often enough it becomes infused with your energy; that the past never leaves us; that there's always atmosphere to consider;[31] that you can wound air as cleanly as you can wound flesh.

In this way, the Dream House was a haunted house. You were the sudden, inadvertent occupant of a place where bad things had happened. And then it occurs to you one day, standing in the living room, that you are this house's ghost:[32] you are the one wandering from room to room with no purpose, gaping at the moving boxes that are never unpacked, never certain what you're supposed to do. After all, you don't need to die to leave a mark of psychic pain. If anyone is living in the Dream House now, he or she might be seeing the echo of you.

---

31. Bennett Sims has a wonderful horror story called "House-Sitting." You have never forgotten this paragraph: "You are not being superstitious, you do not think. It simply stands to reason. For it would be like sleeping in a house where a family has been slaughtered: whether or not you believe in ghosts, there is the atmosphere to consider." It spoke to you, as an agnostic who still can feel when the air in an enclosed space is not quite right.
32. Thompson, *Motif-Index of Folk-Literature*, Types E402.1.1.1, Ghost calls; E402.1.1.2, Ghost moans; E402.1.1.3, Ghost cries and screams; E402.1.1.4, Ghost sings; E402.1.1.5, Ghost snores; E402.1.1.6, Ghost sobs.

# *Dream House as* Chekhov's Trigger

A few days after the incident at the bowling alley, and the day before you are to return to Iowa, she asks if you want to go to a concert at a local bar. You don't—you've hated live music for years, its many demands on your body and your bedtime—but you are afraid to admit that, so you go. This is your first mistake that day. You meet friends there. You buy a beer but sip from it only occasionally, because you want to be able to get in her car and drive at a moment's notice. It's a Chicago band, JC Brooks & the Uptown Sound, and they're actually all right. You sit through a set before you begin to feel exhausted. Being exhausted is your second mistake.

"I need to go home," you tell her softly, leaning into her ear. "I'm so tired, and my flight is kind of early tomorrow."

She seems pleasantly relaxed. "Do you want me to come home with you?" she says.

You relax—this response seems so normal. This is your third mistake.

"I don't care," you say. "If you're having a good time, I can take your car and leave you money for a cab. Or you can come home with me. It's up to you, my love."

"You don't care?" she says.

"Yeah," you say. "Either way is fine."

"So you don't care about me. You don't care whether I come or go."

"That's not what I meant. I just meant—"

"You don't care whether I live or die," she says.

Inside you, something stumbles to the edge of a precipice, falls off.

At the car, she tells you to let her drive.

"No," you say. "No. You're drunk. I won't."

"Give me the keys or I will kill you," she says. She is kidding, probably. You no longer appreciate the joke.

"If I give you the keys, you'll kill us both."

She gets into the passenger seat. The whole way home, you keep waiting for her to dart over the barrier between you and grab the steering wheel. Instead, she closes her eyes.

You walk inside with her screaming at your back. You are calm now. You've learned from the last time. You're already stronger.

In the bedroom you strip off your clothes, then go into the bathroom, lock the door. The shower hotter than you can stand. You are warmed immediately; the sound reminds you of a storm.

Then she's there. Maybe you didn't lock the door properly, maybe you didn't lock it at all—and she is still screaming. She rips the shower curtain down from its rings. You back up. You aren't wearing your glasses so she is just this fuzzy pale mass and her mouth is a red hole. The water falls between you.

"I hate you," she says. "I've always hated you."

"I know," you say.

"I want you to leave this house right now."

"I can't. I don't have my car. My flight is tomorrow."

"Leave this house or I will make you leave."

"I'll sleep on the floor. I'll leave first thing. You won't even know I'm here."

You slide down to the floor of the bathtub, sobbing, and she walks away. You sit there until the water hitting your body is icy. After a few minutes like that, you reach over and turn the handle to off, shivering.

She comes into the bathroom again. When she gets close to you, reaches toward you, you realize she is naked.

"Why are you crying?" she asks in a voice so sweet your heart splits open like a peach.

# Dream House as Soap Opera

She doesn't remember, she tells you before you go to sleep. She remembers being at the bar, and then crouching over you naked. Everything in between is darkness.

# *Dream House as* Comedy of Errors

The next day, you wake up next to her. You pack, and try to convince her to get moving, because she has the car and you have a flight to catch. She is sullen, angry, snaps at you when you remind her that the airport is over an hour away. She takes her time. Puts on her makeup. Drives, for the first time in her life, very slowly.

When you get to the airport, the security line is long, and the TSA agent confiscates your metal water bottle, which you have forgotten to empty. As you pull your heavy suitcase through the airport, you start to cry because of the water bottle, except it's really not the water bottle, and a kindly employee with crimped hair—in 2012!—stops to ask if you're all right. You feel terrible about thinking that thing about her hair; also you sort of want to hug her. And you want to cry and explain that the TSA agent stole your favorite water bottle because he wouldn't let you drink its contents, because perhaps he believed that the bottle contained the liquid from a bomb and by drinking it you would turn into that same bomb, or probably he was just on a power trip because his face didn't change when you begged him to let you keep what you already owned, and also you're afraid you're going to miss your flight because your girlfriend spent her time this morning putting on her face, an expression you've always found sort of funny and vaguely sexist but that now just strikes you as horrifyingly ominous, because it suggests that she has one face and needs to put on another, and you saw underneath it last night, when you were so afraid and cowering, and she was screaming, and you were hiding from her, hiding from the woman who once told you she loved you and wanted to have children with you and called you the most beautiful and sexy and brilliant woman she'd ever met, you had to hide from her in a bathroom with a lock on the door, and if your family found out they'd probably think it proved every idea they've ever had about lesbians, and you wish she was a man because then at least it could reinforce ideas people had about men, and how she probably wouldn't understand but the last thing queer women need is bad fucking PR, and then you feel bad because for all you know this airline employee could be queer, she could understand.

You collapse into your airplane seat with minutes to spare, the last person to board the plane. You are sweaty from running, and you are crying, and you keep sucking snot back up into your nose. Your seatmate is a businessman in a charcoal-gray suit who is definitely regretting not springing for first class, and he keeps looking over at you. And as the ground gets farther and farther away you swear to yourself that you're going to tell someone how bad it is, you're gonna stop pretending like none of these things are happening, but by the time the ground is coming toward you again you are already polishing your story.

# *Dream House as* Demonic Possession

You have always been interested in demon and possession narratives, no matter how cheesy or silly they are. It's the perfect intersection of your morbid curiosities and the remnants of your religious upbringing; a reminder of a time when you believed in that sort of thing.

After she blames those nights on a kind of amnesia, you do research while she mopes around. She feels bad, so bad, she says. There is remorse there, true remorse, and yet sometimes you catch her composing her face into sadness. You google memory loss, sudden onsets of rage and violence. The internet gives you nothing, except one article about how it has been shown that heavy marijuana use can, theoretically, trigger an onset of schizophrenia, if one were already genetically prone to it. This is terrifying; you feel deeply for her. You try to present your various theories, but she scoffs at all of them. She hasn't been smoking much pot, she says. She doesn't have schizophrenia. She says it with such disdain you begin to wonder if you'd exaggerated the events of that trip, whether perhaps you are remembering them wrong.

This is not to say that you seriously consider demonic possession. You are a modern woman and you don't believe in God or any accompanying mythologies. But isn't the best part of a possession story that the inflicted can do and say horrific things for which they'll receive carte blanche forgiveness the next day? "I did what? I masturbated with a crucifix? I spit on a priest?"

That's what you want. You want an explanation that clears her of responsibility, that permits your relationship to continue unabated. You want to be able to explain to others what she's done without seeing horror on their faces. "But she was possessed, see." "Oh well, that happens to everyone at one time or another, doesn't it?"

At night, you lie next to her and watch her sleep. What is lurking inside?

## *Dream House as* Naming the Animals

Adam had one job, really. God said, "See this fuzzy thing? And that scaly thing there, in the water? And these feathery things, flying through the air? I really need you to give them names. I've been making the world for a week and I'm exhausted. Let me know what you decide."

So Adam sat there. What a puzzler, right? It's obvious to us, now, that that is a squirrel and that is a fish and that is a bird, but how was Adam supposed to know that? He wasn't just newly born, he was newly created; he didn't have years of life experience to support this creative enterprise, or anyone to teach him about it. When I think about him, just sitting there with his brand-new fist under his brand-new chin, looking vaguely perturbed and puzzled and anxious, I feel a lot of sympathy. Putting language to something for which you have no language is no easy feat.

# *Dream House as* Ambiguity

In an essay in *Naming the Violence*—the first anthology of writing by queer women addressing domestic abuse in their community—activist Linda Geraci recalls a fellow lesbian's paraphrasing Pat Parker to her straight acquaintance, "If you want to be my friend, you must do two things. First, forget I am a lesbian. And second, never forget I am a lesbian."[33] This is the curse of the queer woman—eternal liminality. You are two things, maybe even more; and you are neither.

Heterosexuals have never known what to do with queer people, if they think of their existence at all. This has especially been the case for women— on the one hand, they seem like sinners in theory, but with no penis how do they, you know, *do it*? This confusion has taken many forms, including the flat-out denial that sex between women is even possible. In 1811, when faced with two Scottish schoolmistresses who were accused of being lovers, a judge named Lord Meadowbank insisted their genitals "were not so formed as to penetrate each other, and without penetration the venereal orgasm could not possibly follow." And in 1921 the British Parliament voted against a bill that would have made illegal "acts of gross indecency between females." Why would an early twentieth-century government be so progressive? "The interpretation of this outcome offered by modern history," writes academic Janice L. Ristock, "is that lesbianism was not only unspeakable but 'legally unimaginable.'"

But this inability to conceive of lesbians has darker iterations too. In 1892, when Alice Mitchell slit her girl-lover Freda Ward's throat in a carriage on a dusty Memphis street—she was enraged that Freda had, with the encouragement of her family, dissolved their relationship—the papers hardly knew

---

33. Legal scholar Ruthann Robson calls this a "dual theoretical demand," and adds, "the demand, of course, is in many cases more than dual. As Black lesbian poet Pat Parker writes in her poem *For the white person who wants to know how to be my friend*: 'The first thing you do is forget that i'm Black / Second, you must never forget that i'm Black.'"

what to do with themselves. In her book *Sapphic Slashers*, Lisa Duggan writes, "Reporters found it difficult to sketch out a clear plot or strike a consistent moral pose: was Alice a poor, helpless victim of mental disease, or was she truly a monstrous female driven by masculine erotic and aggressive motives? . . . A love murder involving two girls presented an astonishing and confusing twist that confounded the gendered roles of villain and victim."[34] The story was simultaneously salacious and utterly baffling. They were . . . engaged? Alice had given Freda a ring, along with promises of love and devotion and material support. Should they execute her for murder, or put her in a hospital for her unnatural passions? Was she a scorned lover or a madwoman? But to be a scorned lover, she'd have to be—they'd have to be—?

"I resolved to kill Freda because I loved her so much that I wanted her to die loving me," Alice wrote in a statement her attorneys provided to the press, sounding every bit the possessive boyfriend from a Lifetime original movie. "And when she did die I know she loved me better than any human being on earth. I got my father's razor and made up my mind to kill Freda, and now I know she is happy."

The jury chose madwoman, and Alice spent the rest of her life in the Western State Insane Asylum in Bolivar, Tennessee.

Even when sex between women was, in its own way, acknowledged, it functioned as a kind of unmooring from gender. A lesbian acted like a man but was, still, a woman; and yet she had forfeited some essential femininity.

The conversation about domestic abuse in lesbian relationships had been active within the queer community since the early 1980s, but it wasn't until 1989, when Annette Green shot and killed her abusive female partner in West Palm Beach after a Halloween party, that the question of whether such a thing was possible was brought before a jury and became one for the courts.

---

34. It should be noted that Alice Mitchell was hardly the first woman to create such public confusion over her gender as it related to both her passions and her shocking act of violence. In 1879, when Lily Duer shot her friend Ella Hearn for rejecting her love, a headline in the *National Police Gazette* read in part, "A Female Romeo: Her Terrible Love for a Chosen Friend of Her *Own Alleged Sex* [emphasis mine] Assumes a Passionate Character." Sometime before the murder, a witness reported an exchange in which Lily said, "Ella, why will you not walk out with me? Do you not love me?" "Oh, yes, I love you," Ella responded, "but I am afraid of you."

Green was one of the first queer people to use "battered woman syndrome" to justify her crime. The idea of the battered woman[35] was brand-new—it had been coined in the '70s—but both *abuse* and *the abused* meant only one thing: physical violence and a white, straight woman (Green is Latina), respectively. The baffled judge eventually allowed Green's defense, but only after insisting on renaming it "battered person syndrome," despite the fact that both the abuser and the abused were women. Regardless, it was not successful; Green was convicted of second-degree murder. (A paralegal who worked with Green's attorney told a reporter that "if this had been a heterosexual relationship," she would have been acquitted.)

All of this contrasts sharply with the way narratives of abused straight (and, usually, white) women play out. When the Framingham Eight—a group of women in prison for killing their abusive partners—came into the public eye in 1992, people were similarly uncertain about what to do with Debra Reid, a black woman and the only lesbian among them. When a panel was convened to hear the women's stories to consider commuting their sentences, Debra's lawyers did their best to leverage the committee's inherent assumptions and prejudices by painting her as "the woman" in the relationship: she cooked, she cleaned, she cared for the children. The attorneys believed, rightly, that Debra needed to fit the traditional domestic abuse narrative that people understood: the abused needed to be a "feminine" figure—meek, straight, white—and the abuser a masculine one.[36] That Debra was black didn't help her case; it worked against the stereotype. (In another early lesbian abuse case, in which a woman gave her girlfriend a pair of shiny black eyes, the

---

35. It should be noted that the word *battered* (as in: battered wife, battered woman, battered lesbian), while woefully imprecise and covering only a fraction of abuse experiences, was the preferred term in this era. It is, of course, a specific legal term with specific legal implications, and I have never thought of myself as a "battered" anyone. The fact that the expression persisted for so long, despite the fact that the lesbian conversation in particular focused on many kinds of abuse that were not explicitly physical, is the perfect example of how inadequate this conversation has been—discouraging useful subtlety. (Other ways in which the conversation remains inadequate: devaluing the narratives of nonwhite victims, insufficiently . addressing nonmonosexuality, rarely taking noncisgendered people into account.)
36. In a 1991 article about a white lesbian in Boise, Idaho, who successfully used "battered-wife syndrome" as a defense for killing her abusive girlfriend, the reporter emphasized that the defendant was a "diminutive 4-foot-10." The prosecutor in the case speculated that the reason for the acquittal was that the abused wife "seemed more heterosexual," and the abuser "more 'lesbian.'"

prosecutor acknowledged that while she was grateful for and surprised by the abuser's conviction, she believed that the fact that the defendant was butch and black almost certainly played into the jury's willingness to convict her.)

The queer woman's gender identity is tenuous and can be stripped away from her at any moment, should it suit some straight party or another. And when that happens, the results are frustratingly predictable. Most of the Framingham Eight had their sentences commuted or were otherwise released, but not Debra. (The board said that she and her girlfriend had "participated in a mutual battering relationship"—a common misconception about queer domestic violence—even though it had never come up during the hearing.) She was paroled in 1994, the second-to-last member of the group to achieve some measure of freedom. An ABC *Primetime* report about them barely talked to or about Debra compared to the other women. The Academy Award–winning short documentary about the Framingham Eight—*Defending Our Lives*—didn't include Debra at all.

The sort of violence that Annette and Debra experienced—brutally physical—or that Freda experienced—murder—is, obviously, far beyond what happened to me. It may seem odd, even disingenuous, to write about them in the context of my experience. It might also seem strange that so many of the domestic abuse victims that appear here are women who killed their abusers. *Where,* you may be asking yourself, *are the abused queer women who didn't stab or shoot their lovers?* (I assure you, there are a lot of us.) But the nature of archival silence is that certain people's narratives and their nuances are swallowed by history; we see only what pokes through because it is sufficiently salacious for the majority to pay attention.

There is also the simple yet terrible fact that the legal system does not provide protection against most kinds of abuse—verbal, emotional, psychological—and even worse, it *does not provide context.* It does not allow certain kinds of victims in. "By elevating physical violence over the other facets of a battered woman's experience," law professor Leigh Goodmark wrote in 2004, "the legal system sets the standard by which the stories of battered women are judged. If there is no [legally designated] assault, she is not a victim, regardless of how debilitating her experience has been, how complete her isolation, or how horrific the emotional abuse she has suffered. And by creating this kind of myopia about the nature of domestic violence, the legal system does battered women a grave injustice." After all, in *Gaslight*, Gregory's only actual crimes are murdering Paula's aunt and the attempted theft of her property. The core of the film's horror is its relentless domestic abuse, but that abuse is emotional and psychological and thus completely outside of the law.

Narratives about abuse in queer relationships—whether acutely violent or not—are tricky in this same way. Trying to find accounts, especially those that don't culminate in extreme violence, is unbelievably difficult. Our culture does not have an investment in helping queer folks understand what their experiences *mean*.

When I was a teenager, there was this girl in my sophomore-year English class. She had luminous gray-green eyes and a faint smattering of freckles across her nose. She was a little swaggery and butch but also loved the same movies I did, like *Moulin Rouge* and *Fried Green Tomatoes*. We sat diagonally from each other and, every day, talked until our teacher threatened to separate us.

I liked her in a way that made me excited to go to class, but I didn't understand why. She was such a good friend and so fun and so smart I wanted to rise out of my seat and grab her hand and yell, "To hell with Hemingway!" and haul her out of class; all to some end I couldn't quite visualize. From the corner of my eye, I stared at her freckles and imagined kissing her mouth. When I thought about her, I squirmed, tormented. What did it mean?

I had a crush on her. That's it. It wasn't complicated. But I didn't realize I had a crush on her. Because it was the early 2000s and I was just a baby in the suburbs without a reliable internet connection. I didn't know any queers. I did not understand myself. I didn't know what it meant to want to kiss another woman.

Years later, I'd figured that part out. But then, I didn't know what it meant to be afraid of another woman.

Do you see now? Do you understand?

## *Dream House as* Undead

I think about Debra Reid so much—incarcerated, unpardoned—how power-less she must have felt. Even after Jackie was gone, she was still there. When Debra was on trial for her murder, Debra's brother brought her a dress to wear. Her first thought was, "Oh God, Jackie going to kill me if she saw me with this one."

# *Dream House as* Sanctuary

The night she chased me in the Dream House and I locked myself in the bathroom, I remember sitting with my back against the wall, pleading with the universe that she wouldn't have the tools or know-how to take the doorknob out of the door. Her technical incompetence was my luck, and my luck was that I could sit there, watching the door test its hinges with every blow. I could sit there on the floor and cry and say anything I liked because in that moment it was my own little space, even though after that it would never be mine again. For the rest of my time in the Dream House, my body would charge with alarm every time I stepped into that bathroom; but in that moment, I was the closest thing I could be to safe.

When Debra Reid was eventually released on parole, she had to stay in prison longer than she needed to because securing housing was a condition of her release and she was having difficulty doing so. She told an interviewer, "I just want to get an apartment and turn my own little doorknob and use my own bathroom and eat my own food."

I can't get Debra or her doorknob out of my mind. I hope she got what she needed.

## *Dream House as* Double Cross

This, maybe, was the worst part: the whole world was out to kill you both. Your bodies have always been abject. You were dropped from the boat of the world, climbed onto a piece of driftwood together, and after a perfunctory period of pleasure and safety, she tried to drown you. And so you aren't just mad, or heartbroken: you grieve from the betrayal.

# *Dream House as* Unreliable Narrator

When I was a child, my parents—and then, learning from their example, my siblings—loved to refer to me as "melodramatic," or, worse, a "drama queen." Both expressions confused and then rankled me. I felt things deeply, and often the profound unfairness of the world triggered a furious, poetic response from me, but while that was cute when I was a toddler, neither thing—feeling, responding to feeling—aged well. Ferocity did not become me. Later, retelling stories about this dynamic to my wife, my therapist, the occasional friend, filled me with incandescent rage. "Why do we teach girls that their perspectives are inherently untrustworthy?" I would yell. I want to reclaim these words—after all, melodrama comes from *melos*, which means "music," "honey"; a drama queen is, nonetheless, a queen—but they are still hot to the touch.

This is what I keep returning to: how people decide who is or is not an unreliable narrator. And after that decision has been made, what do we do with people who attempt to construct their own vision of justice?

# *Dream House as* Pop Single

A year before I was born, the band 'Til Tuesday, led by Aimee Mann, came out with the single "Voices Carry." The breathy, haunting song about an abusive relationship was a top-ten hit in the United States. In the music video—which was in heavy rotation in the early days of MTV—the boyfriend is, for lack of a better word, ridiculous. A meathead in gold chains and a muscle shirt, he delivers his aggressively banal dialogue with the subtlety of an after-school special.

Throughout the video, he dismantles Aimee piece by piece. At first, he compliments her music and her new hair—punky and platinum, with a rattail. Later, in a restaurant that looks like it was borrowed from a sitcom set, he removes her elaborate earpiece and replaces it with a more traditional earring before playfully chucking her under the chin. There is a shot of Mann behind a gauzy curtain, her face pressed into it with desperation, which cuts to her leaving for band practice. Here he confronts her on the steps of their brownstone; when he grabs her guitar case, she tears out of his grasp.

When she returns, he scolds her for her lateness. "You know, this little hobby of yours has gone too far. Why can't you for once do something for me?" When she speaks for the first time—"Like what?" she asks, tilting her chin upward in a challenge—he attacks her, pushing her against the stairs and forcibly kissing her.

At the end of the video, they are sitting in a theater audience at Carnegie Hall. The boyfriend puts his arm around a now-polished Mann—sitting quietly, strung with pearls—before discovering her intact rattail and curling his lip in disgust. Mann begins to sing—softly at first, and then louder as she tears a stylish fascinator off her head. Then she stands up and is screaming, she is scream-singing—"He said 'Shut up' / He said 'Shut up'"—and everyone is turning to look at her. This final scene, Mann said in an interview years later, was inspired by Hitchcock's *The Man Who Knew Too Much*, when

Doris Day's character lets loose a bloodcurdling scream during a symphony performance, to foil an assassination.

Long after the video came out, in 1999 the song's producer revealed that the initial demo of the song had used female pronouns—in the original version, Mann was singing about a woman. "The record company was predictably unhappy with such lyrics," he wrote, "since this was a very powerful, commercial song and they would prefer as many of its components as possible to swim in the acceptable mainstream. I wasn't certain what to think about the pressure to change the gender of the love interest, but eventually thought that it didn't matter any to the impact of the song itself. Would a quasi-lesbian song have had any effect on the liberation of such homosexuals, then as now several difficult steps behind the gays on the path towards broad social acceptance? I don't think so, but it was hard to judge at the time.

"If there is nothing social to be gained," he continued, "there's little point in risking that people might lose the main plot and be confused by something that might be peripheral to them. Maybe better to pull them in, subversively, as the best pop music does. How many more people are now sympathetic to gay people's issues because they responded to gay artists who didn't obviously fly the flag but expressed universal human sentiments that appealed to all? We respond to a song's humanity first, and that is what matters."

Twenty-seven years later—decades into her solo career—the pretense was dropped. Mann released an album, *Charmer*, which included the song "Labrador." The music video was a shot-for-shot remake of "Voices Carry," with the triteness heightened for comedic effect. The introduction—in which a greasy, boorish director admits he tricked Mann into doing the remake against her will—is genuinely funny. But the song itself is just as sad as "Voices Carry," if not more so: the speaker can't help but return to her abusive lover, doglike, over and over again.

"I came back for more," Mann sings. "And you laughed in my face and you rubbed it in / Cause I'm a Labrador / And I run / When the gun / Drops the dove again." The song opens addressed to someone Mann calls "Daisy."

Despite all of this—the suppressed representation, the hackneyed '80s weirdness of the video—"Voices Carry" portrays verbal and psychological abuse in a clear and explicable way. The mania of abuse—its wild emotional shifts, the eponymous cycle—is in the very marrow of the music: dampened, minor-inflected verses without a clear key resolving into a shimmering major chorus before locking back down again. It is not the ironically upbeat prettiness of the Crystals' "He Hit Me (and It Felt Like a Kiss)"—produced in 1963 by Phil Spector, who later murdered actress Lana Clarkson for spurning his advances—though that is its own musical metaphor. Both songs, despite the darkness of their subject, are catchy and endlessly singable.

And I do. Endlessly sing them, that is. Every time I reread this chapter while writing this book, "Voices Carry" was in my head—and my voice—for days afterward. While working on the final draft, I took a break to stand on a beach in Rio de Janeiro watching blue-green waves curl in toward the shore. Around me people were playing soccer and dogs were running into the surf chasing after sticks and the light was amber-soft, and I realized I was singing it. *Hush hush*, I sang to no one, *keep it down now*.

# Dream House as Half Credit

When I was a child, my father told me that if I ever was struggling to answer a question on a test, I should, instead, write down everything I knew about the topic. I took this advice seriously. Where I had doubt, I'd fill the space with what I remembered, what I knew to be true, what I *could say*. I waxed poetic on those scenes in a novel I could visualize clearly, instead of striving to evoke the ones I couldn't. I recorded everything I knew about a particular lab experiment when I couldn't correctly balance equations on my exam. When I couldn't explain how particular historical moments shifted the tide of major world events, I wrote down the little stories I did remember.

Let it never be said I didn't try.

## *Dream House as* Exercise in Style

It would make sense if, during the time in the Dream House, your work suffered. Why not? You were miserable; you spent what probably added up to weeks or months of your life crying and snotting and howling in agony.

But instead, your creativity explodes. You are brimming with ideas, so many that you sign up for six workshops in your last semester of school. You begin to experiment with fragmentation. Maybe "experiment" is a generous word; you're really just unable to focus enough to string together a proper plot. Every narrative you write is smashed into pieces and shoved into a constraint, an Oulipian's wet dream—lists and television episode synopses and one with the scenes shattered and strung backward. You feel like you can jump from one idea to the next, searching for a kind of aggregate meaning. You know that if you break them and reposition them and unravel them and remove their gears you will able to access their truths in a way you couldn't before. There is so much to be gained from inverting the gestalt. Back up, cross your eyes. Something is there.

You will spend the next few years of your career coming up with elaborate justifications for the structure of the stories you were writing at the time— telling them to young readers in classrooms and audiences at bookstores; once, to a tenure-track job search committee. You say, "Telling stories in just one way misses the point of stories." You can't bring yourself to say what you really think: I broke the stories down because I was breaking down and didn't know what else to do.

# *Traumhaus as* Lipogram

It's hard, saying a story without a critical part. Thinking you can say what
you want as you want to, but with a singular constraint. Loss of the function
of a particular orthographic symbol—it's a situation, hmm? A critical loss.
Not just a car with bad paint, a lamp with a crack, sour milk. A car that
can't stop. A lamp that sparks. Milk cut with shit. A woman hid my *thing*
and I can't find it again. That's just how it is. I cannot find what's missing.
I am trying and trying, and I cannot; as I fail, I shrink. I shrink down into
dirt, wood, worms.

It is an awful thing, that missing symbol. Folks *know*. Folks can pick
up on words of rock. Folks will know you for your wounds, your missing
skin. Folks say nothing but *Why didn't you go / Why didn't you run / Why
didn't you say?*

(Also: *Why did you stay?*)

I try to say, but I fail and fail and fail. This is what I did not know until
now: this constraint taints. It is poison. All day and night, until I ran, I was
drinking poison.

# Dream House as Hypochondria

You tell her she has to go to therapy or else you're going to leave her. Sullen, she agrees.

She does go, for a while. The first morning, you make her coffee and breakfast, so that she's ready to head out into the world. You feel like a mother on her child's first day of school. You sit there in your underwear and robe, contemplating the winter morning from the plate-glass window in her kitchen.

She returns in a cheery mood, holding a second coffee; her nose and the tops of her ears blushing with winter.

"What did the therapist say?" you ask. "I know I shouldn't be asking, I just think—"

"We're still getting to know each other," she says. "It's too early to say."

Things get better for a little bit. They really do. She is attentive, kind, patient. She brings you treats—little foods, dips and things, your favorite—and leaves them for you to find when you wake up. A few weeks later, she tells you over the phone that she's not going to continue therapy. "It's too much time," she says. "I'm really fucking busy."

"It's one hour a week," you say, gutted.

"Besides, he says I'm totally fine," she says. "He says I don't need therapy."[37]

"You threw things at me," you say. "You chased me. You destroyed everything around me. You have no memory of any of it. Doesn't that alarm you?"[38]

---

37. Thompson, *Motif-Index of Folk-Literature*, Type X905.4, The liar: "I have no time to lie today"; lies nevertheless.
38. Thompson, *Motif-Index of Folk-Literature*, Type C411.1, Taboo: Asking for reason of an unusual action.

She is silent. Then she says, "I've got lots of things to do. You don't understand how hard I work."

You remember your promise, to leave her if she doesn't get help. But you don't push the issue. You will never talk about it ever again.

## *Dream House as* Dirty Laundry

One day she asks, *Who knows about us?* It becomes a refrain. It's strange—in some past generation this could have meant so many things. Who knows we're together? Who knows we're lovers? Who knows we're queer? But when she asks, the unspoken reason is awful, deflated of nobility or romance: Who knows that I yell at you like this? Who's heard about the incident over Christmas?

She never says exactly that, of course; she just wants to know who you're talking to, who she should be avoiding, who she shouldn't bother to try to charm. Every answer enrages her. When you tell her, "No one," she calls you a liar. When you say, "Just my roommates," her eyes go flat and hard as flint.

# *Dream House as* Five Lights

In the sixth season of *Star Trek: The Next Generation*, Captain Jean-Luc Picard is captured by the Cardassians during a secret mission to Celtris III. Early on in the second episode of the two-episode arc, the Cardassians use a truth serum to interrogate Picard on the details of his mission.

Gul Madred ostensibly wants cooperation; information about the defense strategy for the Minos Korva planetary system. When the serum does not give him the results he desires, he implants a device in Picard's body that, when activated, produces excruciating pain. "From now on, I will refer to you only as 'human,'" Madred tells him. "You have no other identity." They strip Picard naked, hang him from his wrists, and leave him there overnight.

In the morning, Madred is unctuous, measured, unflaggingly polite. He drinks from a thermos like a weary bureaucrat. He turns on a string of lights above him, flooding Picard with illumination. Picard flinches; holds his arm like a wounded velociraptor. Madred asks him how many lights he can see.

"Four," Picard says.

"No," Madred replies. "There are five."

"Are you quite sure?" Picard asks.

Madred presses the button on the device in his hand; Picard buckles, staggers, and drops to the ground in agony. The scene is a pastiche of one from *1984*, but there are also some beats lifted, very lightly, from *The Princess Bride*. Madred is inordinately fond of his machine. *That was the lowest possible setting.*

"I know nothing about Minos Korva," Picard says.

"But I've told you that I believe you. I didn't ask you about Minos Korva. I asked how many lights you see."

Picard squints upward. "There are four lights."

Gul Madred sighs like a disappointed parent. "I don't understand how you can be so mistaken."

Picard squints against them and says, "What lights?" He spasms so hard his body leaps from the chair, strikes the floor.

Lying on the floor, Picard mumble-sings a French folk song from his childhood. "Sur le pont d'Avignon, on y danse, on y danse." *On the bridge of Avignon, we're all dancing, we're all dancing.*

"Where were you?" Madred asks.

"At home. Sunday dinner. We would all sing afterward."

Madred opens the door and tells Picard he may go. But as Picard prepares to leave, Madred tells him he'll torture Dr. Crusher instead. Picard returns to his chair.

"Are you choosing to stay with me?" Madred asks.

Picard is silent.

"Excellent," Madred says. "I can't tell you how pleased this makes me."

Later, Madred feeds Picard. Boiled taspar egg, "a delicacy," he says. When cracked open, it is an undulating, gelatinous mass with an eye at its center. Picard sucks the contents from the shell. Madred has his own meal; shares a story of his own childhood as a street urchin in Lakat, on the Cardassian homeworld.

"In spite of all you have done to me," Picard says with clarity, "I find you a pitiable man."

Madred's cordial attitude vanishes. "What are the Federation's defense plans for Minos Korva?" he shouts.

"There are four lights!" Picard says.

Gul Madred turns on the device, and Picard begins writhing. "How many do you see now?"

Picard screams, weeps, sings. *On the bridge of Avignon, we're all dancing, we're all dancing.*

• • •

Back on the *Enterprise*, the crew has negotiated Picard's release. In the final scene between Picard and Madred, Picard grabs the device that controls the pain, smashes it against a table. Madred calmly tells him it doesn't matter; he has many more.

"Still," Picard says, "it felt good."

"Enjoy your good feelings while you can. There may not be many more of them." Madred goes on to explain that a battle has commenced, and the *Enterprise* is "burning in space." Everyone will assume you've died with them, Madred says, and so you will stay here forever. "You do, however, have a choice. You can live out your life in misery, held here, subject to my whims. Or you can live in comfort with good food and warm clothing, women as you desire them, allowed to pursue your study of philosophy and history. I would enjoy debating with you; you have a keen mind. It's up to you. A life of ease, of reflection and intellectual challenge. Or this."

"What must I do?" Picard says.

"Nothing, really," Madred says. He glances upward, like he's looking for rain before stepping out from under an awning. "Tell me . . . how many lights do you see?"

Picard looks up. He is unshaven, unkempt, covered in a glaze of sweat. His face is a rapidly shifting picture of bafflement and denial, of confusion and agony.

"How many? How many lights?" Madred repeats. Off-screen, a door opens, and Madred's face gets a little frantic. "This is your last chance. The guards are coming. Don't be a stubborn fool. How many?" It is the first time he's seemed weak; exhibited a real need.

Something in Picard's face shatters. He screams: "There—are—four—lights!"

Every time I watch this climax, something inside me grinds a little, like the unglazed edges of a broken mug being shoved together. It is not a triumphant scream. It is broken, humiliating. It cracks like a boy's. The final word, *lights*, is practically oatmeal in his mouth.

Later, safe on the *Enterprise*, Picard talks with Counselor Troi about his experience. "What I didn't put in the report," he tells her, "was that, at the end, he gave me a choice between a life of comfort or more torture. All I had to do was to say that I could see five lights when, in fact, there were only four."

"You didn't say it?" Troi asks.

"No. No," he says. "But I was going to. I would have told him anything. Anything at all. But more than that, I believed that I could see five lights." His gaze rests, lost, in the middle distance.

# *Dream House as* Cosmic Horror

*Evil* is a powerful word. You use it once, and it tastes bad: metallic, false. But what other word can you use for a person who makes you feel so powerless?

Lots of people in the world have made you feel powerless. Run-of-the-mill bullies; both of your parents, and most adults, when you were a child; unflinching bureaucrats at the DMV, the post office. A doctor who didn't believe you were sick, approximately two minutes before you projectile vomited against the wall. A cadre of nurses who pried your arms away from your body to take your blood when they thought you had cancer. (You didn't have cancer, but they never did figure out why you spent so much of your childhood cramping with agony.)

But did any of them seem to enjoy it? Did any of them make you feel complicit in your own suffering? You've outgrown parents and bullies. You've railed against the everyday tyrants to friends; you chastised the doctor while dropping a long line of sour saliva down to the floor; you fought those nurses as hard as if they were trying to murder you.

*Sick* seems more appropriate, but it too tastes bad. It feels too close to *disordered*, which is a word your oldest and dearest friend, who had become very religious after childhood, used when you came out to her. It was over email but you flinched anyway, and before the end of the next paragraph—which explained that she was sort of relieved you hadn't said you had a crush on her—you were already crying.

# *Dream House as* Barn in Upstate New York

Many years later, I wrote part of this book in a barn on the property of the late Edna St. Vincent Millay. I didn't know I was writing the book yet; it would take two more summers to realize it was a book about a house that was not a house and a dream that was no dream at all. But I sketched out scenes and jotted down notes and did a lot of mental excavation staring at the wall of the barn.

A few weeks in, while hiking out in the woods, I came upon what looked like a mound of garbage. When I got closer, I realized what it was: a huge pile of broken and discarded bottles of gin and morphine, where Edna's erstwhile housekeeper had taken the empties and left them.

There was something horrifying about the mountain of glass. I had just finished Edna's biography, wherein I'd learned that weeks after her husband died, she fell to her own death in her house, on the stairs, likely in a haze of intoxication. Was it a terrible accident? Suicide? Everybody has a theory. The biography made me angry. Edna treated her lovers, male and female alike, with no small amount of cruelty. She was talented but arrogant; brilliant but profoundly selfish.

And yet, there among the trees, seeing the measure of her pain, the proportions of her problems, I felt a stab of sympathy. It couldn't have been easy to be married to her, but it couldn't have been easy to be her, either.

One day, a bird slammed into my studio window. I was sitting on a yoga ball and tumbled backward in terror. Almost every residency I've had since, I've found at least one stunned bird sprawled on the ground outside my workspace. I learned: they never see the glass coming. They only see the reflection of the sky.

# *Dream House as* Shipwreck

In New York that winter, when you walk too slowly for her taste, she abandons you at a storage container craft fair in Brooklyn. You stand there with your suitcase and your puffy down coat, and she tells you as she walks away that maybe you should go back to your parents' house in Allentown if you can't take the city.

(This is, you will recognize later, a pattern: she loves to walk away from you in places where you know no one, where you have no power, where you can't simply get up and go somewhere. Over the course of your relationship she will walk away from you in New York a total of seven times.)

You sit down on a bench and numbly try to buy a bus ticket on your phone, but your phone's storage is full and your screen does not respond properly to your finger. When you look up she is actually gone, and you panic, because you don't know New York, and not only do you not know New York, you hate New York, and you have too many bags and no money for a taxi and you don't even know the difference between uptown and downtown. In every direction walk New Yorkers: so confident, so cosmopolitan. You think, they are not the kind of people who get abandoned by their girlfriends at twee craft fairs.

You cry so hard that a tall woman with dreadlocks gets up from her storage container and comes over to you. She sits on the bench and puts her arm around your shoulder, and asks if she can do anything to help. You hiccup and wipe your nose with your hand, and tell her no, no, you're just having a bad day, and she crosses back to her container to fetch something.

When she returns, she hands you a tiny box of cone incense and a carved wooden incense holder. "For your new year," she says, and you want to believe she's right—that even though your suffering feels eternal, unrelenting, the new year is full of promise, and it is coming fast.

# Dream House as Mystical Pregnancy

Every television show you watched in your twenties included some kind of mystical pregnancy. Every interesting female character needs one, or so the showrunners seem to think. Vampires get pregnant with magical mortals; comatose women give birth to gods and empathic starfleet officers to mystic energy; time-traveling companions discover they've been flesh avatars for months, and their actual body is somewhere far away and about to give birth. One woman wakes up on her wedding day to discover herself massively pregnant, courtesy of an alien.

You are thinking of these episodes when you begin to experience pregnancy symptoms in the Dream House. You vomit into the toilet, you feel swollen and out of sorts. The two of you have talked about a child for so long—a little girl, Clementine, hair poufy like a Q-Tip, like hers—that you abandon all reason and wonder if you could be pregnant. You have had so much sex, and the intensity between you feels as real as anything. You consider saying to her, "Ha! I'm sick like I'm pregnant, isn't that weird?" But you are terrified—of the radical body modification that is pregnancy, the dangers of childbirth, the unforgiving nature of motherhood, and—most importantly—of what she'll accuse you of. What she'll do afterward.

You drink ginger ale, you lie down for a long time, you forgo food for an evening under the pretense of having snacked, which you definitely did not do. You cannot be pregnant, you cannot be pregnant, you literally absolutely could not be pregnant under any circumstances.[39] You take a pregnancy test

---

39. Thompson, *Motif-Index of Folk-Literature*, Types T511.1.3, Conception from eating mango; T511.1.5, Conception from eating lemon; T511.2.1, Conception from eating mandrake; T511.2.2, Conception from eating watercress; T511.3.1, Conception from eating peppercorn; T511.3.2, Conception from eating spinach; T511.4.1, Conception from eating rose; T511.5.2, Conception from swallowing worm (in drink of water); T511.5.3, Conception from eating louse; T511.6.1, Conception from eating woman's heart; T511.6.2, Conception from eating finger-bones; T511.7.1, Conception after eating honey given by lover; T511.8.6, Conception from swallowing a pearl; T512.4, Conception

anyway, like an idiot, and of course it's negative because you haven't had a penis anywhere near your body in years. You are afraid she'll find the test, so you put it in a Ziploc bag and throw it out in someone's trash can on the street after she's gone to class.

_____

from drinking saint's tears; T512.7, Conception from drinking dew; T513.1, Conception through another's wish; T514, Conception after reciprocal desire for each other; T515.1, Impregnation through lustful glance; T516, Conception through dream; T517, Conception from extraordinary intercourse; T521, Conception from sunlight; T521.1, Conception from moonlight; T521.2, Conception from rainbow; T522, Conception from falling rain; T523, Conception from bathing; T524, Conception from wind; T525, Conception from falling star; T525.2, Impregnation by a comet; T528, Impregnation by thunder (lightning); T532.1.3, Impregnation by leaf of lettuce; T532.1.4, Conception by smell of cooked dragon heart; T532.1.4.1, Conception after smelling ground bone-dust; T532.2, Conception from stepping on an animal; T532.3, Conception from fruit thrown against breast; T532.5, Conception from putting on another's girdle; T532.10, Conception from hiss of cobra; T533, Conception from spittle; T534, Conception from blood; T535, Conception from fire; T536, Conception from feathers falling on woman; T539.2, Conception by a cry.

# *Dream House as* Choose Your Own Adventure®

You wake up and the air is milky and bright. The room glows with a kind of effervescent contentment, despite the boxes and clothes and dishes. You think to yourself: *this is the kind of morning you could get used to.*

When you turn over, she is staring at you. The luminous innocence of the light curdles in your stomach. You don't remember ever going from awake to afraid so quickly.

"You were moving all night," she says. "Your arms and elbows touched me. You kept me awake."

If you apologize profusely, go to page 163.

If you tell her to wake you up next time your elbows touch her in your sleep, go to page 164.

If you tell her to calm down, go to page 166.

"I'm so sorry," you tell her. "I really didn't mean to. I just move my arms around a lot in my sleep." You try to be light about it. "Did you know my dad does the same thing, the sleeping damsel swoon? So weird. I must have—"

"Are you really sorry?" she says. "I don't think you are."

"I am," you say. You want the first impression of the morning to return to you; its freshness, its light. "I really am."

"Prove it."

"How?"

"Stop doing it."

"I told you, I can't."

"Fuck you," she says, and gets out of bed. You follow her all the way to the kitchen.

Go to page 168.

"Baby, if this ever happens in the future, you can always wake me up and I'll go to the couch, I promise. I really don't mean to do it. I don't have any memory of it. I can't control how I move in my sleep."

"You're such a fucking cunt," she says. "You never take responsibility for anything."

"All you have to do is wake me up," you say, a kind of incoherent desperation zipping through your skull. "That's it. Wake me up and tell me to move or sleep on the couch and I will do it, I swear to you."

"Fuck you," she says, and gets out of bed. You follow her to the kitchen.

Go to page 168.

Here you are; a page where you shouldn't be. It is impossible to find your way here naturally; you can only do so by cheating. Does that make you feel good, that you cheated to get here? What kind of a person are you? Are you a monster? You might be a monster.

END. Go to page 177.

Are you kidding? You'd never do this. Don't try to convince any of these people that you'd stand up for yourself for one second. Get out of here.

END. Go to page 177.

You shouldn't be on this page. There's no way to get here from the choices given to you. You flipped here because you got sick of the cycle. You wanted to get out. You're smarter than me.

Go to page 171.

Breakfast. You scramble some eggs, make some toast. She eats mechanically and leaves the plate on the table. "Clean that up," she says as she goes to the bedroom to get dressed.

If you do as you are told, go to page 169.

If you tell her to do it herself, go to page 166.

If you stare mutely at the dirty plate, and all you can think about is Clara Barton, the feminist icon of your youth who had to teach herself how to be a nurse and endured abuse from men telling her what to do at every turn, and you remember being so *angry* and running to your parents and asking them if women still got told what was right or proper, and your mom said "Yes" and your dad said "No," and you, for the first time, had an inkling of how complicated and terrible the world was, go to page 171.

As you're washing the dishes, you think to yourself: Maybe I could tie my arm down somehow? Maybe put a tack on my forehead? Maybe I should be a better person?

Go to page 171.

You shouldn't be on this page. There's no way to get here from the choices given to you. Did you think that by flipping through this chapter linearly you'd find some kind of relief? Don't you get it? All of this shit already happened, and you can't make it not happen, no matter what you do.

Do you want a picture of a fawn? Will that help? Okay. Here's a fawn. She is small and dappled and loose-legged. She hears a sound, freezes, and then bolts. She knows what to do. She knows there's somewhere safer she can be.

Go to page 171.

That night, she fucks you as you lie there mutely, praying for it to be over, praying she won't notice you're gone. You have voided your body so many times by now that it is force of habit, reflexive as a sigh; it reminds you of your first boyfriend who fucked you while watching porn—how he rutted and rutted and then every so often lifted the remote to rewind something you couldn't see. (Once you turned your head over the lip of the bed and saw a tangle of upside-down limbs and your brain couldn't make sense of them; you never looked again.) You would just lie there silently, watching his face move over you. It was like being unfolded beneath the yawn of the planetarium as a kid: the sped-up rotation of the earth, the movement of the stars over you, the constellations melting into and out of being as a distant, disembodied voice told some ancient story to help make sense of it all.

You shudder and moan with precision. She turns off the lights. You watch the darkness until the darkness leaves you; or you leave it.

To sleep, go to page 175.

To dream about the past, go to page 172.

To dream about the present, go to page 174.

To dream about the future, go to page 173.

The first time it happened—the first time she yelled at you so much you were crying within thirty seconds from waking, a record—she said, "The first ten minutes of the day, I'm not responsible for anything I say." This struck you as poetic. You even wrote it down, sure you would find a place for it: in a book, maybe.

Go to page 175.

It's going to be all right. One day, your wife will gently adjust your arm if it touches her face at night, soothingly straightening it while kissing you. Sometimes you will wake up just enough to notice; other times, she'll only tell you in the morning. It's the kind of morning you could get used to.

Go to page 175.

You shouldn't be here, but it's okay. It's a dream. She can't find you here. In a minute you're going to wake up, and everything is going to seem like it's the same, but it's not. There's a way out. Are you listening to me? You can't forget when you wake up. You can't—

Go to page 175.

You wake up and the air is milky and bright. The room glows with a kind of effervescent contentment, despite the boxes and clothes and dishes. You think to yourself: *this is the kind of morning you could get used to.*

When you turn over, she is staring at you. The luminous innocence of the light curdles in your stomach. You don't remember ever going from awake to afraid so quickly.

"You were moving all night," she says. "Your arms and elbows touched me. You kept me awake."

If you apologize profusely, go to page 163.

If you tell her to wake you up next time your elbows touch her in your sleep, go to page 164.

If you toss back the blankets from your body and hit the floor with both your feet and tear through the house like it's Pamplona, and when you get to the driveway your car keys are already in your hand and you drive away with a theatrical squeal of the tires, never to return again, go to page 176.

That's not how it happened, but okay. We can pretend. I'll give it to you, just this once.

Turn to page 177.

# *Dream House as* L'appel du Vide

In the pit of it, you fantasize about dying. Tripping on a sidewalk and stumbling into the path of an oncoming car. A gas leak silently offing you in your sleep. A machete-wielding madman on public transit. Falling down the stairs, but drunk, so you flop limb over limb like a marionette and feel no pain. Anything to make it stop. You have forgotten that leaving is an option.

# *Dream House as* Libretto

My middle school music teacher showed a film version of *Carmen* to the class, the really famous one with Julia Migenes where she keeps hiking up her skirt during the Habanera. He was probably just trying to give you all a bit of culture, but all my classmates took away from the screening and the ensuing discussion was that Carmen was a prostitute who didn't shave under her arms, and by extension, by thirteen-year-old logic, I must also be a prostitute who doesn't shave under her arms. They asked me about both of these things over and over again. Already smarting after a decade of Carmen Sandiego jokes, I was ready to abandon my name altogether.

When Carmen sings, she tells the men who surround her that love is a fickle thing, and they need to beware. Don José gives himself over to her, loses himself in her. When she leaves at the end, he begs her not to go. She tells him that she was born free and she will die free.

Then he stabs her, and she dies.

Confessing his crime to the gathering crowd, he throws his body on Carmen's corpse and howls, "Ah, Carmen! Carmen, my adored one!" As though he hadn't just killed her with his own hands.

# *Dream House as* Sci-Fi Thriller

One night, John and Laura ask if you want to watch a movie with them: *Flatliners*. Julia Roberts, Kiefer Sutherland, Oliver Platt, Kevin Bacon: all med students playing with the edge of death. You are so excited; you remember seeing this movie on TV as a teenager, and you are ready for the shot of nostalgia. You all make drinks, sit down together.

As soon as the movie starts, you fall asleep, your legs slung over the arm of the couch.

You are tired. You are tired and the room is warm and dark and John and Laura are there, breathing gently next to you. You remember the opening—silhouetted statues in the half-light of sunset and a sweeping, dramatic choral arrangement, and Kiefer Sutherland announcing that it is a good day to die. And then you are out. You do not dream. When you wake up, the movie is over; you've missed the entire thing. And yet you feel so content there, in that space, in the moment after waking, and before you remember your cell phone.

When you crash into your bedroom, it is lying there at the end of its charger. Still and traitorous. When you pick it up, there are missed calls, text messages. You call her back, shaking, your pectoral muscles twisting into fists of anxiety.

"Hello." You can hear the smolder of rage in her voice.

"I'm so sorry," you begin to explain, breathlessly. "We just—"

"Who were you fucking?"

You feel your chest pulling inward.

"No one," you say. Then, "Wait, wait, I can—"

You run into the living room, where John and Laura are sprawled content as cats. John sees your face, stands up.

"I can prove it to you," you say to her. "John and Laura are here, I can give them the phone, they can tell you, they can prove I wasn't with anyone else, we were just watching a movie—"

If you live into eternity, if you live until the sun crashes into the earth, you will never forget the expression on John's face, the way he slumps forward and looks flattened with grief. He shakes his head very slightly, though it's not clear if he's refusing the task or refusing the reality where the task is being offered to him.

"No," she says. The smoke in her voice clears immediately. "No, no need."

You talk to her after that, almost certainly, but you have no memory of the conversation. The moment when you woke up on that couch—before you remembered the phone, remembered your entire life—was one of the sweetest from that year. That tiny pocket of safety and oblivion. Whiskey, breath, bodies. Credits crawling up the dark.

# *Dream House as* Déjà Vu

She says she loves you, sometimes. She sees your qualities, and you should be ashamed of them. If only you were the only one for her. She'd keep you safe, she'd grow old with you, if she could trust you. You're not sexy, but she will have sex with you. Sometimes when you look at your phone, she has sent you something stunningly cruel, and there is a kick of fear between your shoulder blades. Sometimes when you catch her looking at you, you feel like she's determining the best way to take you apart.

# *Dream House as* Murder Mystery

Lightning flashes, the power dies, and when the electricity comes back on again a dinner guest is folded over the dessert course with a dagger in her back. The handle of the blade is inlaid with precious gems, but her tiara is missing. When the undercover detective reveals herself—the plucky reporter, of course!—the mystery deepens: the cost of the gems in the handle of the knife far outweighs the value of the stolen tiara, whose diamonds were merely glass. Who among them would give up a tool of such immeasurable value to take something so worthless? And so boldly, in front of so many people?

The plucky reporter paces on the Persian carpet in front of the suspects. Was it Heathcliff, the brawny dockworker turned mob boss? Ethan, the foppish social climber with eyes like the distant radiance of Mars? Samson, the experimental artist with a murky and enigmatic past? The reporter crosses dozens of times in front of a slight, blonde woman sitting in the corner, but never includes her on the list. The blonde woman is leaning back with flinty cool, following the action. She nods and listens, and every so often tilts her chin in the direction of the plucky reporter and lets loose a dazzling smile.

The plucky reporter turns to Samson with a trembling, gloved finger. Samson stands to defend himself. Ethan begins shouting, Heathcliff glowers. And no one pays attention to the blonde woman, who stands and walks toward the corpse of the dinner guest. She grips the blade with both hands and pulls it out like King Arthur deflowering the stone.

The body of the dinner guest, whose eyes are wide and wet with betrayal, lifts with the movement and then slams back down on the place setting, lemon cake squashed against her bosom. The blonde woman wipes the blood off the blade onto the dinner guest's dress and replaces it in her purse. Everyone continues to argue as she walks out the front door and into the night.

# IV

The trouble with letting people see you at your worst isn't that they'll remember; it's that you'll remember.

—Sarah Manguso

## *Dream House as* Stopgap Measure

She gets into your MFA program and will leave the Dream House to come to Iowa City. She talks about moving in with you. You coo with excitement over the phone, but when you hang up you feel like you did when you were a kid and your brother launched a baseball into your nose: warm blood down the back of your throat; milk, and metal.

# *Dream House as* the Apocalypse

According to some students of eschatology, 2012 was supposed to be the end of the world. And it was, in a way.

But the end did not come as fire or flood. No glittering comet struck our planet. No virus leapt from continent to continent until bodies lay strewn in the streets. The flora of the world did not grow to overtake our buildings. We did not run out of oxygen. We did not vanish or burst into dust. We did not all wake up with blood soaked into our pillows. We did not watch a beam from an alien ship carving trenches into the earth's crust. We did not turn into animals. We did not starve or use up all of our potable water. We did not trigger a new ice age and freeze to death. We did not choke to death in a self-induced smog. We didn't get sucked through a wormhole. The sun did not overtake us.

At the end of the world, the park was beautiful, hot. The grass was a little long. The trees were punctuated with birds.

## *Dream House as* Surprise Ending

"I'm in love with someone else," she says. The two of you are sitting in an Iowa City park next to a baseball diamond after a friend's baby shower, and you don't understand how the conversation even arrived at this point. The grass is crowded with dandelions, and you remember, suddenly, that game you played as a kid, yellow-chinned, in love.

"What?" you say.

"With Amber," she says. You think of Amber—a classmate of hers at Indiana, willow-thin and redheaded, with a soft, mousy voice. "We kissed once, drunkenly, and I realized that I loved her."

You stare at her, fast-forwarding through a mental film of every time she'd accused you of merely looking at other people the wrong way. She meets your gaze for a moment and then looks away. She slings her arm over the back of the bench, like she's going to bring you in close. She doesn't.

You get in your car, drive to a distant street, and pull over. You don't have the space in your brain to cry. You pick up your phone and see that, on Freecycle, someone is giving away catalog cards from a defunct library. You drive to a local Panera, take a stack of cards from a very nice woman who is probably wondering why you look like you've been forced to eat dog shit at gunpoint. Back at your house you calmly add the pile of cards to your scrap collection because you think you'd like to make a collage.

Very late, your girlfriend—or is she?—appears at your house and says she has to get back to Bloomington. Where has she been this whole time? She doesn't say, but she kisses you. "I think we're meant to get through this," she says. "Don't worry. Promise me you won't worry."

# *Dream House as* Natural Disaster

I get bad heartburn. It's the Zoloft, which takes the edge off my anxiety but brings along a bunch of awful side effects, like a good friend who can't shed a bad lover. Every so often, I take my nightly meds and within a few minutes feel as though a hot poker has been shoved down my esophagus. I chew antacids and walk to the bathroom. Often the pain, or the force of the neutralization, makes me vomit. I become, functionally, everyone's favorite science fair project.

When I bend over the toilet, I think a lot about how my heart is a volcano, like that quote from Kahlil Gibran. It's dumb but it moved me—spoke to my shifting tectonic plates—and I wrote it down on a Post-it I stuck on my desk: "If your heart is a volcano how shall you expect flowers to bloom in your hands?" It stayed there until a bad day, working on this book, when I suddenly loathed the quote with every ember of my being and crumpled it up and threw it away.

Reader, do you remember that ridiculous movie *Volcano*, the one with Tommy Lee Jones? Do you remember how they stopped eruption in the middle of downtown Los Angeles? They diverted it with cement roadblocks and pointed fire hoses at it, and rerouted the lava to the ocean, and everything was fine? Sweet reader, that is not how lava works. Anyone can tell you that. Here is the truth: I keep waiting for my anger to go dormant, but it won't. I keep waiting for someone to reroute my anger into the ocean, but no one can. My heart is closer to Dante's Peak of *Dante's Peak*. My anger dissolves grandmas in acid lakes and razes quaint Pacific Northwest towns with ash and asphyxiates jet engines with its grit. Lava keeps leaking down my slopes. You should have listened to the scientist. You should have evacuated earlier.

So, Kahlil Gibran. I know what he's saying, but even rhetorically he is making exactly the wrong point. The fact is, people settle near volcanoes because the resulting soil is extraordinary, dense with nutrients from the ash. In this dangerous place their fruit is sweeter, their crops taller, their flowers more radiant, their yield more bountiful. The truth is, there is no better place to live than in the shadow of a beautiful, furious mountain.

# *Dream House as* the Pool of Tears

You talk on the phone, but soon she stops picking up, stops responding to your texts. "If you don't want me to worry," you tell her when she finally answers, "if you want me to feel safe, you're not doing a very good job." Your body feels huge, swollen, as though it is pressed into the room's corners and your limbs are growing out of the windows.

"I don't care," she says, so softly that you know it's true.

"Are you still seeing her?" you ask.

You cry and cry.[40] You cry into your phone, flood it with saltwater. It stops working.[41] So she breaks up with you over Skype instead. Her face is pinched and regretful.

"I still want to be your friend," she says.

When it is over, you stare at your dark, dead phone; a rectangle of black glass. It grows in your hand, larger and larger, and you discover that, instead, you are shrinking. By the time the realization hits you, you are three feet tall. One foot. Six inches. And then, up to your chin in saltwater. You wonder if you have somehow fallen into the sea. "And in that case," you think, "no one will come and get me." You soon make out, though, that you are in the pool of tears that you had wept when you were nine feet high.[42]

"I wish I hadn't cried so much!" you say as you swim about, trying to find your way out. "I shall be punished for it now, I suppose, by being drowned in my own tears! That will be a queer thing, to be sure! However, everything is queer today."

---

40. Thompson, *Motif-Index of Folk-Literature*, Type C482, Taboo: weeping.
41. Thompson, *Motif-Index of Folk-Literature*, Type C967, Valuable object turns to worthless, for breaking taboo.
42. Thompson, *Motif-Index of Folk-Literature*, Type A1012.1, Flood from tears.

# *Dream House as* Mrs. Dalloway

On the night of the day she breaks up with you, you are meant to host a party for one of your professors after her reading.

To hang Christmas lights around the dining room, you drag a thrift-store bookcase over to the wall and stand on it. You are reaching up and up when you hear the particle board give. You don't fall off, you fall *through* it, and that's where John and Laura find you: standing in the ruins of the bookcase with blood trickling down your legs, sobbing gushily.[43] (At the ocean at your feet, a Dodo paddles by, waves to you.) You are embarrassed that you thought a cheap, piece-of-shit set of shelves could bear your weight; you are embarrassed about your blood, its redness, the way it is just coming out of you with no concern for anyone's feelings. You are embarrassed to be throwing a party in this state, embarrassed to be alive.

"What happened?" John asks, and when you don't answer he repeats the question, and then he leads you to the couch and asks Laura to get some Band-Aids. Laura rolls up your leggings and cleans the cuts with hydrogen peroxide. John sits next to you, resting his wide hand between your shoulder blades, anchoring your shuddering skeleton.

John calls one friend, who calls another, and soon all the people you've spent a year and a half not confiding in have shown up on your doorstep. They find you lying across the couch and get to work like the mice in *Cinderella*— sweeping, cleaning, making shopping lists.

Someone asks you if you've eaten, and someone else answers for you ("Nope"), so someone else orders a pizza. You sit there, a glass of water in your hand, as they all crisscross in front of you, being kinder than you think you deserve.

---

43. Thompson, *Motif-Index of Folk-Literature*, Type C949.4, Bleeding from breaking taboo.

The doorbell rings. As someone signs for the pizza there is a blur of color and light, and suddenly something small and warm is in your lap. It's a puppy, a tiny, wiggling hound puppy with massive paws and a whipping tail. When you get a good look at her, you realize she belongs to your neighbor, who is also coincidentally your therapist (Iowa City!). You pick up the puppy, who is writhing with inarticulable joy, slathering your face in sloppy, flat-tongued kisses. You are crying as you carry the puppy outside, where you can hear your therapist and his wife calling her name. You go to the fence, and your therapist apologizes—they'd been loading up the car and she'd gotten away. Your therapist does not say anything about your shiny red nose and tearstained face. "I'll see you next week," you whisper as you bundle the vibrating creature over the fence. Home once again, the puppy gives you one last kiss, darting across the barrier like a clandestine lover.

You rally enough to dress and light the tea candles. The party hums around you, a machine that doesn't need you at all. A tremendous success.

# *Dream House as* Apartment in Chicago

You and your friends decide to get out of town, and you arrange a trip to Chicago. You left a broken phone behind, but this does not stop you from touching your pocket reflexively, wondering if she's been trying to call you.

Even through your grief, you appreciate the trip: you sleep on the couch of the sublet you rented together and only wake up because your friend Tony gently crab-claws your foot poking out from beneath a blanket. When you look around the room, all of your friends sleeping so close to each other, like kittens, and you want to curl into a pile with all of them.

Still, you cry at meals, you cry in the streets. When you break off for small-group activities, you go with Ben and Bennett. You love them both, and mostly you love how they will not emote at you or ask you how you're feeling. You go to the Art Institute of Chicago and spend a lot of time in two places: the Thorne Miniature Rooms and Ivan Albright's *That Which I Should Have Done I Did Not Do (The Door)*. Both fill you with a queer pleasure; both make you cry. One makes you feel immortal, godlike: as if you are a time-traveling spirit, hunched up in the corners of nineteenth-century English drawing rooms and sixteenth-century French bedrooms and eighteenth-century American dining rooms, watching the lives of the mortals play out in miniature dioramas. The other makes you feel small, as if you are prostrate before death's flickering veil. Small, and then even smaller, and soon you find yourself paddling in your own tears, again. You hear something splashing about in the pool a little way off, and you swim nearer to make out what it is. At first, you think it must be a walrus or hippopotamus, but then you remember how small you are now, and you soon find that it is only a mouse that has slipped in just like you.

"Would it be of any use, now," you think, "to speak to this mouse? Perhaps he's a Cuban mouse, come over during the Ten Years' War." (For, with all your knowledge of history, you have no very clear notion how long ago anything has happened.) So, you begin: "¿Dónde está el gato malo?" which is the first complete Spanish sentence you can think of. The Mouse suddenly leaps out of the water, quivering with fright. "Oh, I beg your pardon!" you cry, afraid you have hurt the poor animal's feelings. "I quite forgot you didn't like cats, good or bad."

"Not like cats!" shouts the Mouse. "Would you like cats if you were me?"

"Well, perhaps not," you say soothingly. "Don't be angry about it. And yet I wish you could meet my cat; I think you'd take a fancy to it if you could only see her. She is such a dear thing," you go on, half to yourself, as you swim lazily about in the pool, "and she sits purring so nicely by the fire, licking her paws and washing her face—and she's such a capital one for catching mi—oh, I beg your pardon!" you cry again, for the Mouse is swimming away from you as hard as it can and is making quite a commotion. You call softly after it, "Mouse, dear! Do come back, and we won't talk about cats!"

When the Mouse hears this, it turns around and swims slowly back to you: its face is quite pale (with passion, you think), and it says in a low, trembling voice, "Let us get to the shore, and then I'll tell you my history, and you'll understand why I am afraid of cats."

It is high time to go anyway, for the pool is getting crowded with the birds and animals that have fallen into it: there is a Duck and a Dodo (Amy Parker's "trusting, extinguished bird"), a Lory and an Eaglet. And among them, every stranger who has ever seen you cry in public is doing the breast-stroke. You turn from their pity and lead the way; the whole party swims to the shore. At the water's edge, the creatures and the strangers disperse into the streets of Chicago.

When you arrive home, there's a message in your inbox: "I've made a mistake."

# *Dream House as* Sodom

Like Lot's wife, you looked back, and like Lot's wife, you were turned into a pillar of salt,[44] but unlike Lot's wife, God gave you a second chance and turned you human again, but then you looked back again and became salt and then God took pity and gave you a third, and over and again you lurched through your many reprieves and mistakes; one moment motionless and the next gangly, your soft limbs wheeling and your body staggering into the dirt, and then stiff as a tree trunk again with an aura of dust, then windmilling down the road as fire rains down behind you; and there has never been a woman as cartoonish as you—animal to mineral and back again.

---

44. Thompson, *Motif-Index of Folk-Literature*, Type C961.1, Transformation to pillar of salt for breaking taboo.

## *Dream House as* Hotel Room in Iowa City

She emails you to tell you that she is staying in a hotel room in Iowa City, and will you come see her? You say no, no, but then you go anyway.

She says she is in town to see you, that she wants to be with you, and you bring a box of her things to leave with her but end up staying instead. You scream at her, and cry. At some point, there is a knock on the door. You open it, and a slow-speaking, square-headed Iowa City bro stands on the other side. He has a strange, eerie smile. He says that the two of you should come party with his friends, do you want to come on over? They have booze, and other things. You don't learn what the other things are, you just close the door. You stand there for a second, then flip the deadbolt.

She comes up behind you, to hug you. You pull away so hard you smash into the door. You turn and slide down to the floor and she says, "Shhhh, shhhh," and you beg her not to touch you, but she does. She leans in to your head. "Did you change your shampoo?" she asks, and you nod because you have. You have sex with her because you don't know what else to do; you only speak the language of giving yourself up. "This will work," she says to you as she touches you. "Amber means nothing to me. When I think about her, I feel sick. This will work, I promise. I love you so much."

The morning after, you go to a restaurant next door. A gorgeous baby coos from the adjacent vinyl booth, and it makes you cry so hard the waitress writes with a blue pen on your Styrofoam box of leftovers: *Have a beautiful day! Maria.* You are startled because she's written your middle name, and you think to yourself that she's sending you a message before you realize it is her first name. You take the box of her things back to your car, drive home.

A week later—after you've convinced yourself that everything is going to be okay and you've gotten a new phone—you run into a woman who asks if your girlfriend has found an apartment yet, since she's been here in town, looking. You are confused, but then later that night, when a friend tells you about a rumor she's heard through the grad-school grapevine—your girlfriend is dating Amber, back in Indiana—you realize so many things all at once: She is not planning on moving in with you. You have made some bad choices.

You call her, tell her what you know. Even here, on this incontrovertible hook, she equivocates so smoothly you can barely see her squirm. It is, she explains, *merely complicated*. She simply has too many wonderful things in her life; she is having difficulty making sense of it all. "I cannot be an attentive girlfriend while I love someone else," she says, finally, and then it is over for good.

# *Dream House as* Equivocation

In Dorothy Allison's short story "Violence Against Women Begins at Home," a group of lesbian friends gathers for a drink and they discuss a bit of community gossip: a pair of women recently broke into another woman's house and trashed it, smashing glass and dishes and destroying her art, which they deemed pornographic. They spray-painted the story's eponymous phrase on her wall. The friends debate police involvement and intragroup conflict mediation; but toward the end of the story, as they are parting ways, the problem crystallizes into a single, telling exchange:

> "Look, do you think maybe we could hold a rent party for Jackie, get her some money to fix her place back up?"
>
> Paula looks impatient and starts gathering up her stuff. "Oh, I don't think we should do that. Not while they're still in arbitration. And anyway, we have so many important things we have to raise money for this spring—community things."
>
> "Jackie's a part of the community," I hear myself say.
>
> "Well, of course." Paula stands up. "We all are." The look she gives me makes me wonder if she really believes that, but she's gone before I can say anything else.

Queer folks fail each other too. This seems like an obvious thing to say; it is not, for example, a surprise to nonwhite queers or trans queers that intracommunity loyalty goes only so far, especially when it must confront the hegemony of the state. But even within ostensibly parallel power dynamics, the desire to save face, to present a narrative of uniform morality, can defeat every other interest.

The queer community has long used the rhetoric of gender roles as a way of absolving queer women from responsibility for domestic abuse. Which is not to say that activists and academics didn't try. When the conversation about queer domestic abuse took hold in the early 1980s, activists gave out fact sheets at conferences and festivals to dispel myths about queer abuse.[45] Scholars distributed questionnaires to get a sense of the scope of the problem.[46] Fierce debates were waged in the pages of queer periodicals.

But some lesbians tried to restrict the definition of abuse to men's actions. Butches *might* abuse their femmes, but only because of their adopted masculinity. Abusers were using "male privilege." (To borrow lesbian critic Andrea Long Chu's phrase, they were guilty of "[smuggling patriarchy] into lesbian utopia.") Some argued that consensual S&M was part of the problem. Women who were *women* did not abuse their girlfriends; proper lesbians would never do such a thing.[47] There was also the narrative that it was, simply, complicated. The burden of the pressure of straight society! Lesbians abuse each other!

Many people argued that the issue needed to be handled within their own communities. Ink was spilled in the service of decentering victims, and abusers often operated with impunity. In an early lesbian domestic abuse trial, a lawyer noted the odd and unsettling detail that most of the time the jury spent behind closed doors was—contrary to what she'd been worried about—the straight jurors attempting to convince the jury's sole lesbian member of the defendant's guilt. When she was later questioned, the lesbian

---

45. Among the myths tackled by the Santa Cruz Women's Self Defense Teaching Cooperative: "Myth: It's only emotional/psychological, so that doesn't count." "Myth: I can handle it—unlike her last three lovers." "Myth: Staying together and working it out is most important." "Myth: We're in therapy, so it'll get fixed now."

46. Actual questionnaire language by researcher Alice J. McKinzie: "Is your abuser present at this festival? If your abuser is at this festival, is she present while you are filling this out? If your abuser is not present while you are filling this out, is she aware that you are filling out this questionnaire? If you answered NO to the question above . . . do you plan to tell her later?"

47. This No True Scotsman fallacy could bend these narratives in every direction conceivable; create a kind of moving goalpost that permitted an endless warping of accountability. In a firsthand account of her abuse in *Gay Community News* in 1988, a survivor wrote: "I had been around lesbians since I was a teenager, and although some of them had troubled relationships, I was unaware of any battering. I attached myself to the comforting myth that *lesbians don't batter*. Much later, when I was 'out' enough to go to gay bars in a town that was liberal enough to tolerate them, I saw that some lesbians did indeed batter. However, I thought they were all of a type—drunks, sexist butches or apolitical lesbians—so I decided that *feminist lesbians don't batter*." Activist Ann Russo put it more succinctly in her book *Taking Back Our Lives*: "I had found it hard to name abuse in lesbian relationships as a *political issue with structural roots*."

juror told the lawyer that she hadn't "wanted to convict a [queer] sister," as though the abused girlfriend was not herself a fellow queer woman.

Around and around they went, circling essential truths that no one wanted to look at directly, as if they were the sun: Women could abuse other women. Women *have* abused other women. And queers needed to take this issue seriously, because no one else would.

# *Dream House as* the Queen and the Squid

Here is a story I learned from a squid:

There was a queen, and she was lonely again. So she summoned all of her counselors, who then summoned all of the personages in the land so she could find a companion of her very own.

The counselors spent much time in deliberation, and after three days behind closed doors they brought her a squid, with no small amount of pomp and pageantry. She was utterly delighted. The squid was everything she had ever wanted: pearlescent and damp, sinewy and intelligent. The squid, in turn, was delighted with her own new situation. She had, from afar, admired the queen, and could hardly believe the queen had chosen her as her own.

At first, their friendship was a magnificent one. They traveled to the edges of the kingdom, and the squid would bring the queen beautiful baubles from tiny sea caves at the coast. The queen took the squid to visit distant dignitaries, and at night they trawled the shadowed halls in search of midnight snacks. It was a companionship defined by its tenderness, and the two were unspeakably happy.

But after a while, the queen grew bored with her companion. Those were difficult times. Sometimes the queen left the squid locked outside her study, and the squid would sit upon the dry, cool stones praying she would be returned to her bowl before her skin turned to paper. And even when the queen and the squid kept each other company, the queen was distant, often cruel. She would flip the squid over and drop little pieces of trash into her gnashing beak. And the queen would scrub whatever surface the squid touched, scolding her for her thoughtless messes. (The squid, as you know, has three hearts, and all of them broke over and over in her time with the queen.)

One night, when the queen was sleeping, the squid decided to gambol about the palace. She found her way to a mop bucket and wheeled herself around the corridors, enjoying the silence. After she had traveled some distance she found herself at the end of a hallway, before a very strange and heavy door. The squid was about to turn around and leave when she heard something.

She opened the door and slid into the dim room.

The smell was terrible. Not the organic stench of death but the wine-dark depths of sorrow—thick and bitter. And the sounds—the squid had never heard anything like that before. The low moan of water draining from a bath; keen wails darting through the room like bright birds.

The squid's large eyes began to adjust to the light. When she realized what she was seeing, she wheeled her bucket as quickly as possible back down the hallway and back to the queen's room.

Some time later, the squid looked out the window and saw that the queen was cavorting with a bear. The bear was beautiful: massive and shaggy and radiant. The squid, heartbroken, knew she could not even begin to compare. When the queen and the bear departed for a picnic, the squid asked a chambermaid to take her into town.

When the queen discovered that her squid was gone, she was enraged. But once her anger receded, she knew what she needed to do. So the queen sat down and wrote the squid a letter.

"My dearest creature," she wrote. "Before I begin, I must ask you to keep an open mind and an open heart about the following missive.

"I love you, and I will *always love you*. The fact that you refuse to come to my chambers, even just as a companion and not as a lover, stills my heart. You seem to believe that the fact that our love has ended means we can never be in proximity to each other, and I beg you to reconsider. I have loved many creatures in my lifetime—a goat, a honeybee, an owl—and despite the fact that our love did not endure, I still see them regularly. We are still friends. Just because I have found happiness in the companionship of a bear *does not mean* that our time together meant nothing.

"I am sorry that things did not work out between us. I have, as I hope you would agree, behaved *honorably* and *beyond reproach*. I am filled with grief and sorrow that you do not believe in amicable partings. I would have thought that you—intelligent creature that you are—would know better.

"The truth is that you have been with me during a very difficult period of my life, and I am sorry that I have not been on my best behavior. But such is love! What we have will transcend this messy business, and we will be in each other's lives forever. Does that not please you? None of this jealousy or betrayal; just a friendship based on mutual trust. I hope one day we can meet each other in some neutral space, our pain limned with understanding, with all of this behind us. I faithfully await your reply."

When the squid did not reply, the queen wrote another letter:

"Sweet squid! The mistakes that I have made number in the thousands, I think. I have spent many days meditating, fasting, abstaining from alcohol, and am now realizing how profoundly I failed you. The truth is, you are my past and my future. I miss you. I wish I could suckle your tentacles and kiss your cool mantle, and that we could travel like we used to. I'm so sorry about the bear. The bear is beautiful and very special in her own right but she is nothing like you. She is still here in the castle but when I pass by her I have a strong desire to turn and run in the opposite direction. It is only you I want, my little cabbage. Not that I want to eat you, ha-ha! I just want you nestled in my stomach for all eternity. Please come back to me. Come back to me and I will pledge myself to you as I knew I should have many months ago. I have been a fool, but please, help me be a fool no longer. Marry me. And when we die our bodies will be scattered in the heavens as twin constellations, the queen and the squid, and no one will have known happiness like ours. I love you, I love you, my sweet darling, I love you. Faithfully and Truly, Your Queen."

After receiving this last letter, the squid began to construct a reply. She spent many hours writing and discarding drafts of letters; some took longer than others. She lamented the use of her ink for such an exhausting and pointless purpose. Eventually, she penned words that satisfied her. She sent her letter off by messenger and then made her way to a local farmer. There, she exchanged coin for a horse and a waterproof bladder that could be suspended from the saddle. The squid slurped into the skin and bade farewell to the town where she had suffered so.

When the letter arrived, the queen opened it with trembling hands.

"My queen," the letter said, "your words are very pretty. And yet they cannot obscure the simple fact that I have seen your zoo."

Here is a story I learned from a bear:

There was a queen, and she was lonely again.

# *Dream House as* Thanks, Obama

Right before the breakup, Barack Obama visits Iowa City. He comes to talk about student debt, and you are a student and you have so many kinds of debt, so you go. Your heart feels like a picked-off scab hot with infection. You get there late and are shuffled into an overflow room, where his speech will be viewable on a screen. You're mad at yourself for being late, sad to be shunted off into another room. It feels, like so many things these days, a sign.

Then, just before the speech starts, Obama comes into the room where you're stewing. The bleachers are crowded but there is room on the top step, a place where you're definitely not supposed to be standing because there is nothing behind it but air. Your strongest friends pull themselves up and help you follow. You look out over the crowd and see the president— your president—walking before the crowd. You've never seen him up close before. He waves and smiles and begins to speak, and the air in front of you glints with smartphone screens.

You close your eyes. You can feel the metal of the bleacher step bending minutely below your feet like a tuning fork, and you think *I am more than six feet from the ground.* It would be so easy to die; a brief moment of faintness; a temporary abandonment of your body's rigor. A man in front of you has a shirt on. "Obama '08: He's ready to go!" *Yes,* you think. *Yes, she is. I know.*

The day you break up for the last and final time is the day Obama announces, publicly, that he supports marriage equality. It is a Wednesday in May 2012. Your little brother's twenty-third birthday. Joe Biden had, unscripted, bumbled into a public statement of support a few days before.

"At a certain point I've just concluded that for me, personally, it is important for me to go ahead and affirm that I think same-sex couples should be able to get married," Obama says in that sweet, thoughtful, politician-y way that irritates the hell out of you and also makes you want to hug him.

The first time you voted for him, in 2008, you woke up to the simultaneous news that he'd won, and that California had rejected the possibility of you marrying a woman. It was a sweet-sour morning; through the fog of a hangover, you watched his victory speech with your roommate. "I'm sorry about Prop 8," she said softly. You shrugged. You celebrated him despite his position on gays marrying because he was the best thing possible at that moment; imperfect in a way that affected you but was generally good for the world. You did not believe this was a battle that would be won in your lifetime, and so you resolved yourself to live in that wobbly space where your humanity and rights were openly debated on cable news, and the defense of them was not a requirement for the presidency. You were already a woman, so you knew. Occupying that space was your goddamned specialty.

Years later, so sad and shattered, you laugh at his statement because you can't think of what else to do. "Great timing," you say to your laptop screen. "Thanks, dude."

You figure it out: you take a Xanax and sleep on and off for days.

## Dream House as Void

It is hard to describe the space that yawns open in your life after she is gone. You have to make yourself leave your phone at home; you have to practice ignoring it. You keep reminding yourself that you are accountable to no one. You try to imagine sex with other people and struggle to visualize it; masturbation is near impossible.[48] You wonder if you will ever be able to let someone touch you; if you will ever be able to reconnect your brain and body or if they will forever sit on opposite sides of this new and terrible ravine.

---

48. Thompson, *Motif-Index of Folk-Literature*, Type C947, Magic power lost by breaking taboo.

# *Dream House as* Unexpected Kindness

You have this really Republican uncle, Nick. Like, really, really Republican. Ann Coulter books on his coffee table, Fox News spewing technicolor paranoia into his living room, and a huge collection of guns that he insists on showing you because he knows it makes you uncomfortable. (You've never been able to explain to him the utter terror you felt the only time you shot a gun: an older guy you were crushing on took you out to a range and you both used a Glock to send old hard drives spinning to the dirt. You tried it because he'd said, "Most women are too small and slight to deal with this kind of kickback, but you're strong and solid, so here you go." You took the gun—because you were flattered by this assessment, because you wanted to sleep with him, because feminism—but then regretted it immediately. You were terrified; you felt like the gun was going to explode in your hand, kill both of you, and afterward you swore you'd never pick one up again. For a long time, that hunk of metal sat on your windowsill, sunlight streaming through the bullet hole. But when you moved you threw it away.)

Nick lives in Wisconsin, and being in the Midwest you see him from time to time. You like him, despite yourself. He might represent everything you loathe, politically speaking, but he's a giant teddy bear and he always calls you his "favorite Democrat," even though you haven't identified that way since college.

The day after the woman from the Dream House breaks up with you for the second time, Nick calls you. He sounds jolly on the phone, explains that he's coming through town on business, and could he swing by for a quick visit? You say sure, then hang up, then immediately begin scolding yourself. Not only are you not out to a man who thinks highly of Bill O'Reilly, but you're a mess. You haven't showered in days. You run around trying to throw yourself together, and an hour later you see his huge car chugging down the street. He gets out, waves to you, and starts up your sidewalk. He is a few feet away when you start sniffling uncontrollably. His face expands with concern. "What's wrong?" he asks.

"Uncle Nick," you say, "I am a lesbian, and my girlfriend just broke up with me." Then the wrecking ball goes clear through the dam, and you begin to bawl.

"Ohhhhh," he says. "Ohhhhh." You are wrapped in his arms; he is hugging you so tight. "Your heart is broken. I understand. Everyone's heart breaks in the same way."

Everyone's heart does not break in the same way, but you know what he means. You both go inside and sit down on the couch. For the next hour, he tells you stories about his various breakups—he's been married three times—and gives you advice. "Join a club," he says. "Take up a new hobby. What about boating? Do you like boating?"

You laugh, and for the first time in what feels like a year, you smile.

# *Dream House as* Memory

You spend the month after the breakup doing unofficial CrossFit with your friend Christa, who is brilliant and kind and pushes you. "You're a natural athlete!" she says admiringly over and over again, and it is hilarious because you are so fat and the furthest possible thing from a natural athlete, but the year's events have given you uncanny focus, and it's true that you have been improving: you can now lightly jog a mile without stopping and deadlift two hundred pounds.

One day, as you drag your aching body to the locker room, you see that you have nine missed calls. They are all from her, the woman from the Dream House, and there are voicemails to match. Suddenly the phone goes off again, vibrating like a maniacal insect, and you almost drop it on the floor. You sprint out to the parking lot. The whole drive home the phone is ringing, ringing. You run into the house where John is reading, and show him the phone.

He leaps into action, attaches his computer to the elaborate speaker system he's set up in your house, and begins to play some sort of chaotic noise metal. He runs around like Mickey from "The Sorcerer's Apprentice," adding his own energy to the noise. "Resist, Carmen, resist!" he cries, slapping the counter with his hands and hitting pans with wooden spoons and amping up the music as loud as it will go.

(In *Angel Street*, when the police sergeant finally makes contact with the tormented, gaslit wife, he tells her firmly, "You are up against the most awful moment in your life, and your whole future depends on what you are going to do in the next hour. Nothing less. You have got to strike for your freedom, and strike now, for the moment may not come again.")

You feel suddenly infused with the discordance, and yell "fuck you" at the phone (which has done nothing but its precise function!) before attempting to figure out how to block her number. You end up googling it, and once it's done, the phone goes silent. But the voicemails are there, and you ask John to turn down the music.

Each one is a little different. Some are steeped in sorrow: *I love you, I miss you*. Others are threatening. *You fucking cunt, pick up this phone right now*. (As if she has forgotten you own a cell phone and not a landline, and you are not standing still in the kitchen listening to her voice on an answering machine while she's leaving her message.) You are so deeply freaked out by this seemingly unhinged sequence, like a bad and offensive movie about a woman with multiple personality disorder, that you try to imagine her leaving the messages—where she might be in the Dream House. You imagine her threatening you in the bedroom, weeping for you in the living room, pledging her undying love in the office. You think it will make you feel better, but it makes you feel worse.

You save the voicemails, in case you need to get a restraining order. When you upgrade your phone a few months later, they are lost.

# *Dream House as* Denouement

You have planned a chat with Val between an end-of-semester barbecue and a house party. You leave the former later than you intend, so when Val calls, you pull over on a shady street. It is so strange to hear her voice, soft and sweet over the phone. You chatter nervously at each other for a few minutes before arriving at a mush of apologies and tears.

"I can't believe you agreed to be in an open relationship," you say to her.

"She cared about you," she says. "I didn't think I had a choice."

"Before that."

"What do you mean?"

"When I met her, she was in an open relationship."

The silence on the end of the line is long and slow.

"What are you talking about?" she asks.

When you arrive at the house party, your friends all stare at you and ask if you're okay.

"I need a drink," you say. "And then I need to tell you a story."

## *Dream House as* Schrödinger's Cat

Was it the arc of the universe? The natural result of centuries, millennia of wrongheaded politics? Was she trained to find you, or were you trained to be found? Was it the fact that you'd already been tenderized like a pork chop by: never having been properly in love, being told you should be grateful for anything you get as a fat woman, getting weird messages that relationships are about fighting and being at odds with each other? The fact that your heart had been broken that one time and you desperately wanted to feel it unbreak? That you felt complete with someone loving you? That you just straight-up loved being desired, desiring someone, coming all the time? That you got addicted to her smell, her voice, her body? That you figured this was what you deserved? The superpredictable result of a religion that pathologized sex but never talked about relationships? Terrible sex ed? Bad timing?

You feel as if there is a box you can open to find the answer, but with the lid closed the answer is all of these things, all at once.

# *Dream House at* Newton's Apple

Early in the summer, this guy drops you a line. When you first got to Iowa, he had flown into town and the two of you spent a weekend in bed together and it was a nice culmination of a few years of light internet flirtation. It turns out he's in town for a conference for work, and he asks if you want to get dinner. You agree, even though you don't really want to see him. You even agree to pick him up from his hotel—his request—although you don't want to do that, either.

Even as you're driving to his hotel, you're thinking about how you're just doing what he's asking you, the same way you'd respond to the woman in the Dream House, even though he's just this random guy. You think about that as you pull up under the awning, as you drive him to the restaurant. He is talking to you. Even as you're responding to him, even as you're ordering and making small talk, you're marveling at the fact that his maleness—the generic fact of it—has as much pull as a carefully curated, long-term abusive relationship. It's as if one scientist spent decades developing a downward-facing propulsion system to get an apple to descend to the ground and another one just used gravity. Same result, entirely different levels of effort.

You refuse to get a drink, pick at your meal. He insists on paying. You drive him back to the hotel. You pull in front of the entrance, and he smiles at you.

"Why don't you park so we can say good-bye?" he asks.

You pull into the parking space around the corner.

"Why don't you walk me inside?" he says. "There's a gorgeous koi pond in the lobby."

He's not wrong. The soaring atrium is breathtaking. It's nicer than any hotel you've ever stayed in. You bend over a bridge and look down at the koi, their muscular bodies the color of warning. You think about how much easier it would be to just sleep with him. He isn't the worst guy in the world. The effort of resisting is exhausting.

"I should go," you say. "I have a thing at eight."

He makes a clucking sound in his throat, smiles.

"Why don't you come on up?" he says.

"I have to go," you say.

He walks you back to your car, and as you fish your keys out of your purse, he kisses you. He keeps kissing you; he grabs your arms, pushes his tongue in your mouth. Your body goes rigid. You don't fight, but you don't respond. You briefly float outside your body and see yourself, the almost comedy of your mismatched libidos. When he pulls away, he does not seem to notice that you can feel nothing at all. He gives you a key card, tells you his room number, in case you change your mind.

On the drive home you pull over near a parking garage and stumble out onto a patch of grass. You drop down into child's pose and take deep, shuddering breaths as the car's emergency signal ticks next to you. The grass catches the copper light: on and off and on again.

# *Dream House as* Sex and Death

In June, you drive from Iowa to San Diego for a genre-writing workshop on the UCSD campus. On the way you stop in Berkeley, where you lived so long ago. You leave your things at a friend's house and meet up with your ex-boyfriend for dinner.

After a few drinks, you tell him about her, about the Dream House. He listens intently, his eyes soft with kindness. It is so good to see him your heart aches. You realize you have missed him so much because what was wrong with you as a couple was so contained, so clear. Even the cosmic agony of his departure felt like a normal (if terrible) part of life, like a broken leg or being fired from a job.

As dinner winds to a close, you ask if he wants to go get a drink. But when you step out onto the street you remember how early things close around there.

"I've got a lot of booze back at my place," he says. The sentence is careful but he's smiling sidelong at you. Your heart and cunt twitch simultaneously. You text your friend, the one you're staying with. *I understand*, she responds. *Have fun. Breakfast tomorrow?*

Your ex-boyfriend gestures to a car on the street; a comically tiny convertible. You laugh, genuinely pleased. "You have a convertible?" It comes out weirdly; you say it again and again, changing inflections. "*You* have a convertible? You have a *convertible*?" You might be a little tipsy already.

"Should I leave the roof down?" he asks.

"Um, *yes*," you say. He starts the engine and you drop the seat back and watch Berkeley and then Oakland this way the whole drive back, the tips of buildings at the circumference of your vision, a sky streaked with clouds with stars in the gaps between them. The car is going so fast that you feel wild, you feel like you could die right now and it would be thrilling. You realize you are laughing, and he goes even faster.

• • •

In his apartment, you scratch his cat's head hard with your fingernails. He makes you a drink. You sit down across from each other.

"I've missed you," he says.

*I've missed myself,* you want to say, but you don't. "I've missed you too," you say. "I mean, I don't miss men, but I did miss you. I'm glad we did this."

You straddle him and kiss him and later, when you are standing in the bathroom doing your best to wash semen out of your hair, he says something from the other side of the door. "What?" you ask, and open it.

"It's gonna be okay," he says. "I mean, you're gonna be okay."

You call him a weirdo and then return to the sink, dunking half your head under the faucet. When you look back in the mirror, you are smiling a little.

You have breakfast with your friend; you tell her about the night before. You feel so good, you say. At peace, or something. The next day, her house burns to the ground. Your friend is fine, but one of her roommate's houseguests is killed in the blaze. You are thinking about fire inspectors examining your hot bones among the cinders as you drive out of town and south through the Central Valley. The air is dry and the traffic terrible, but you can see orchards for miles. The light is gold.

# *Dream House as* Plot Twist

You spend the rest of your time in San Diego writing, drinking scotch, taking long walks down to the beach with your classmates, and pulling massive bullwhips of kelp out of the ocean. You and Val talk every other day. One day, she asks if she can accompany you on your way back to Iowa, when you're done.

You pick her up in LA. She is windswept and beautiful, and the two of you bundle into the car and drive. You blast Beyoncé's "Best Thing I Never Had" as you drive toward the Grand Canyon. You get there near sunset, and you lead her to the edge and you talk about the depth and ancientness of it all. The photo you take there is one of your favorites: Val staring out at the vast expanse of space, carved inch by inch by water and wind and time. Her mouth is hanging open, her dark curls blowing around her face.

A few days later, on a friend's foldout couch in New Mexico, you reach out for each other in the dark. Val asks if she can kiss you, and you say yes.

Every day, you drive and talk about the woman in the Dream House. At night, you curl into each other.

You visit every tourist trap in Roswell, New Mexico. You sleep at a shady motel in southern Colorado, where an elderly couple next door smokes weed that pours through the flimsy shared wall, and signs warn about bears. You drive up a mountain in Rocky Mountain National Park, your tiny car winding up narrow paths and sharp switchbacks until you reach the peak. You visit your cousins and their new baby in Nebraska; the baby's head is stained purple from gentian violet.

You talk about her, the woman in the Dream House, but you also talk about who you were before her, and who you are hoping to be after.

Eventually, you and Val will come to love each other outside this context. You will move in together, get engaged, get married. But in the beginning, this is what holds you together: the knowledge that the two of you are not alone.

# V

Two or three things I know for sure and one of them is that telling the story all the way through is an act of love.

—Dorothy Allison

# *Dream House as* Nightmare on Elm Street

Seven years on and I still dream about it, even though I am four houses/three lovers/two states/one wife past the Dream House; and the dreams aren't terribly unlike those I had when I was a kid, the ones in which I could hear the distant thumping footsteps of some unseen monster. The footsteps never sped up or slowed down but remained horribly, terribly even, and when I'd try to hide (because hiding was all I could do; there never seemed to be the possibility of opening the door and going out into the world beyond the house) there'd be creatures in my way: a skeleton under the bed, a ventriloquist's dummy behind the shower curtain, a zombie in the closet. And while they were terrible, and I had the sense in that dream that I could not share a hiding space with them, I also recognized that they were hiding because they were scared, smaller monsters terrified of that large, unseen thing, and as I ran from room to room the steady footsteps of the oncoming thing never faltered. And so seven years on I am still terrified that if I force myself awake (as I learned to do as a child), she will step out of the dream and into the waking world where I am safe and so far away.

# Dream House as Talisman

When Val and I started dating, I still had a year left in Iowa City. I saw the woman from the Dream House often; on the streets and at bookstores, making the town her own. I had not yet trained my body to resist the nauseated panic those sightings brought me, and so Val got me a vial of angelica root from a store in Salem, Massachusetts. It looked like wood chips, smelled funky and spicy. I bought a locket on a long, burnished chain and tapped the fragments of root into the pendant.

"I do not believe in this," I said.

"Wear it," she said. "Let it work."

So I did. Who knows if it warded anyone off, but here's what it definitely did do: tapped against my breastbone, smelled like bad incense. Every so often, the clasp loosened, and the fragments spilled down my front or into my bra. When I got undressed at night, I'd notice the chamber of it hanging open, waiting to be refilled. It reminded me that Val cared about me, and also that nothing can keep you safe.

# *Dream House as* Myth

When you try to talk about the Dream House afterward, some people listen. Others politely nod while slowly closing the door behind their eyes; you might as well be a proselytizing Jehovah's Witness or an encyclopedia peddler.[49] Kind to you in person, what they say to others makes its way back to you: *We don't know for certain that it's as bad as she says. The woman from the Dream House seems perfectly fine, even nice. Maybe things were bad, but it's changed? Relationships are like that, right? Love is complicated.*[50] *Maybe it was rough, but was it really abusive? What does that mean, anyway? Is that even possible?*

You will never feel as desperate and fucked up and horrible as you do when you hear those things. Once, a woman drunkenly touches your elbow at a party and says, "I believe you," in your ear, and you cry so hard you have to leave. You walk home in the dark over a footbridge and see a fat raccoon waddling up the riverbed.

The raccoon is a trickster; everyone knows that. He doesn't look up, he doesn't speak to you, he just keeps going. But keeping going is a way of speaking. You hear him. He's saying you will fight this fight for the rest of your days.

---

49. Thompson, *Motif-Index of Folk-Literature*, Type C423.3, Taboo: revealing experiences in other world.

50. "Experiencing the ordinary brutality of love does not make one a victim. It makes one an adult," Maureen Dowd wrote of Joyce Maynard, when Maynard published a memoir about how a decades-older J. D. Salinger seduced, abused, and disposed of her when she was eighteen. What, I wonder, is Maureen's definition of *ordinary? Brutality? Love?*

## *Dream House as* Death Wish

Afterward—when she will not stop trying to talk to you or emailing you with flowery apologies on Yom Kippur, and when people do not believe what you tell them about her and the Dream House—you'll wish she had hit you. Hit you hard enough that you'd have bruised in grotesque and obvious ways, hard enough that you took photos, hard enough that you went to the cops, hard enough that you could have gotten the restraining order you wanted. Hard enough that the common sense that evaded you for the entirety of your time in the Dream House had been knocked into you. You have this fantasy, this fucked-up fantasy, of being able to whip out your phone and pull up some awful photo of yourself, looking glazed and disinterested and half your face is covered in a pulsing star. This is, as you said, fucked up: there are probably millions of people on the blunt end of a lover's fist who pray for the opposite, daily or even hourly, and to put that sort of wish into the universe is demented in the extreme.

You will wish for it anyway. Clarity is an intoxicating drug, and you spent almost two years without it, believing you were losing your mind, believing you were the monster, and you want something black and white more than you've ever wanted anything in this world.

# Dream House as Proof

So many cells in my body have died and regenerated since the days of the Dream House. My blood and taste buds and skin have long since re-created themselves. My fat still remembers, but just barely—within a few years, it will have turned itself over completely. My bones too.

But my nervous system remembers. The lenses of my eyes. My cerebral cortex, with its memory and language and consciousness. They will last forever, or at least as long as I do. They can still climb onto the witness stand. My memory has something to say about the way trauma has altered my body's DNA, like an ancient virus.

I think a lot about what evidence, had it been measured or recorded or kept, would help make my case. Not in a court of law, exactly, because there are many things that happen to us that are beyond the purview of even a perfectly executed legal system. But the court of other people, the court of the body, the court of queer history.

In *Cruising Utopia: The Then and There of Queer Futurity*, José Esteban Muñoz writes, "The key to queering evidence, and by that I mean the ways in which we prove queerness and read queerness, is by suturing it to the concept of ephemera. Think of ephemera as a trace, the remains, the things that are left, hanging in the air like a rumor."

That ephemera: The recorded sound waves of her speech on one axis and a precise measurement of the flood of adrenaline and cortisol in my body on the other. Witness statements from the strangers who anxiously looked at us sideways in public places. A photograph of her grip on my arm in Florida, with measurements of the shadows to indicate depth of indentation; an equation to represent the likely pressure. A wire looped through my hair, ready to record her hiss. The rancid smell of anger. The metal tang of fear in the back of my throat.

None of these things exist. You have no reason to believe me.

• • •

"Ephemeral evidence is rarely obvious," Muñoz says, "because it is needed to stand against the harsh lights of mainstream visibility and the potential tyranny of the fact."

What is the value of proof? What does it mean for something to be true? If a tree falls in the woods and pins a wood thrush to the earth, and she shrieks and shrieks but no one hears her, did she make a sound? Did she suffer? Who's to say?

# *Dream House as* Public Relations

And haven't men been gaslighting women, abusing their lovers, harassing their girlfriends, murdering their wives for as long as human history has existed? And isn't their violence always a footnote, an acceptable causality? David Foster Wallace threw a coffee table at Mary Karr and pushed her out of a moving car, but no one ever really talks about it. Carl Andre almost certainly shoved Ana Mendieta out the thirty-fourth-story window of their Greenwich Village apartment and got away with it.[51] In Mexico, William Burroughs shot Joan Vollmer in the head; her death, he said later, made him into a writer. These stories are so common that they are no longer shocking in any meaningful sense; it is more surprising when there is no evidence of a talented man having hurt someone at all. (I confess, I never quite believe it; I just assume those men are better at hiding than most.)

I have spent years struggling to find examples of my own experience in history's queer women. I tore through book after book about the queer women of the past, pen poised over paper, wondering what would happen if they had let the world know they were unmade by someone with just as little power as they. Did Susan B. Anthony's womanizing extend to psychological torment? What did Elizabeth Bishop really say to Lota de Macedo Soares when she'd been drinking heavily? Did their voices crawl with jealousy? Did they hurl inkwells and figurines? Did any of them gingerly touch their bruises and know that explaining would be too complicated? Did any of them wonder if what had happened to them had any name at all?

· · ·

---

51. Andre was tried for, and acquitted of, Mendieta's death. In his 911 call, Andre told the operator, "My wife is an artist, and I'm an artist, and we had a quarrel about the fact that I was more, eh, exposed to the public than she was. And she went to the bedroom, and I went after her, and she went out the window." Whenever Andre has an exhibition, protestors show up. They create outlines of bodies on the ground, as if someone has fallen from a great height. They leave animal viscera smeared on sidewalks. They ask, "¿Dondé está Ana Mendieta?"

I'll never forget the gut punch I felt when one of the first lesbian couples married in Massachusetts got divorced five years later—a kind of embarrassed panic. I was recently graduated, newly out, trying to date women in Berkeley. I remember feeling dread, as though divorces weren't the kind of thing happening all around me at every moment, as if they weren't a complete nonentity. But that's the minority anxiety, right? That if you're not careful, someone will see you—or people who share your identity—doing something human and use it against you. The irony, of course, is that queer folks *need* that good PR; to fight for rights we don't have, to retain the ones we do. But haven't we been trying to say, this whole time, that we're just like you?

It's not being radical to point out that people on the fringe have to be better than people in the mainstream, that they have twice as much to prove. In trying to get people to see your humanity, you reveal just that: your humanity. Your fundamentally problematic nature. All the unique and terrible ways in which people can, and do, fail. But people have trouble with this concept. It's like how, after *Finding Nemo*, people who were ill equipped to take care of them rushed to buy clown fish and how the fish died. People love an idea, even if they don't know what to do with it. Even if they only know how to do exactly the wrong thing.

# *Dream House as* Cabin in the Woods

I went to Yaddo to write this book in full performance mode. I didn't realize it until a few weeks in, when I was midlaugh middinner and, for the first time in ages, heard myself. As a teenager I would have given my eyeteeth for this sense of sureness. I performed as a witch, a socialite. I wore mermaid-cut skirts and silk jumpsuits and elegant, floor-length sequined dresses and faux-fur wraps and black frocks and glittering rhinestone earrings. I didn't hold back on my opinions. I drank wine at dinner and took second helpings and strutted around the grounds. I slept mere feet from where I wrote, in a cabin in the trees. I played Pokémon Go on long walks and vied for control of the property's single gym (located, abstractly, in a grand and elegant fountain at the base of the slope that dropped down from the mansion) with an avatar called "Hornbuckets." It was autumn, and every day leaves and pine needles came down; I was forever picking detritus out of my bra. It got cold, and warm, and cold again. It snowed, but the snow melted the next day. I drove to southern Vermont for a reading on Halloween with a bunch of other writers and blew out a tire on a dark country road on the way home, and as we waited for AAA we sat in the car and told stories about our worst jobs.

In the mansion on the property, the furniture was gathered to the center of the room and draped in sheets. I saw a painting of the dead children, dressed in black. I thought I heard my name in a half whisper, but when I turned around there was no one. "Sound moves weirdly in here," one of the residents explained. The rooms were, in turn, monastic, bombastic. I nursed a crush on a playwright and a nonfiction writer both, rolled my eyes at a sculptor, felt great fondness for badass visual artists who were breaking into the fine arts boys' club before I was born. I talked about supplements with a painter and comforted a composer. Donald Trump was elected president. People cried at the dinner table. Toward the end, I told the story about the Dream House, the funny version: the version where the irony of my relationship with Val and the universality of shitty exes are at the forefront. I kept my eyes open: for deer, for ghosts.

# *Dream House as* Prisoner's Dilemma

Many years later, you stick a memory card into your SLR and find dozens of naked photos of the woman in the Dream House. You jerk involuntarily when the first image comes onto the preview screen.

You remember the afternoon so clearly: how the soft, indirect natural light filtered into the room; how she was naked and pale and lounging, and how her cunt was flushed maroon with blood. (It was either just before fucking or just afterward.) You got down between her knees and took dozens of photos, loving the ombre of her, from white to pink to purple. The memory is not sexual; it is distant and removed, as if you are watching a movie about someone else.

You sit there for a while, thinking about the photos. You could keep them, but there is no reason to, good or bad. You have no desire for black-mail or the kind of revenge they could make possible; you do not find them erotic anymore. (How quickly your desire curdled when you saw her for what she was, like the scene in *The Shining* when Jack Nicholson pulls away from a sexy woman to find a decomposing creature in her place.) They are simply a memory, and as you overwrite the data card, erasing them forever, you feel an irrational twinge of loss.

## *Dream House as* Parallel Universe

You occasionally find yourself idly thinking about how it could have gone right. Or, maybe *gone* isn't the best word, because it suggests that nothing was under anyone's control; the outcome is merely fate, or chaos theory. But assuming she'd been normal, assuming she hadn't homed in on your soft spots, assuming she'd not been shot through with that dark, smoky core of poison, what would have happened? Any number of things. Maybe you and she and Val would have stayed a threesome, a polyamory success story. Maybe you wouldn't have stayed together but you would have remained dear friends, a trio growing old parallel to each other. Or maybe it would have been messy and sad. Sometimes you wish you'd had the chance to find out.

# *Dream House as* Self-Help Best Seller

When it started, I believed I was special. It was a terrible thing to discover that I was common, that everything that happened to me—a crystalline, devastating landscape I navigated in my bare feet—was detailed in books and reports, in statistics. It was terrible because I wanted to believe that my love was unique and my pain was unique, as all of us do. ("Having now described the fiasco with the Professor at length," Terry Castle writes, "I confess, I feel on the one hand a bit embarrassed by its sheer triteness: my own sitting-duckness, my seducer's casebook callousness.") But then I opened book after book about lesbian abuse and saw pseudonymed women regurgitating everything that happened to me. There is a pie chart that encompasses those years of my life. A pie chart!

The first book about lesbian abuse was published the year I was born. Not the most ancient scholarship in the world, but old enough. Why did no one tell me? But who would have told me? I knew so few queer people, and most of them were my age, still figuring things out themselves. I imagine that, one day, I will invite young queers over for tea and cheese platters and advice, and I will be able to tell them: you can be hurt by people who look just like you. Not only can it happen, it probably will, because the world is full of hurt people who hurt people. Even if the dominant culture considers you an anomaly, that doesn't mean you can't be common, common as fucking dirt.

# Dream House as Cliché

We think of clichés as boring and predictable, but they are actually one of the most dangerous things in the world. Your brain can't engage a cliché, not properly—it skitters right over the phrase or sentence or idea without a second thought. To describe an abusive situation is almost certainly to deploy cliché: "If I can't have you, no one can." "Who will believe you?" "It was good, then it was bad, then it was good again." "If I stayed, I would have died." Awful and dehumanizing, and yet straight out of central casting. This triteness, this predictability, has a flattening effect, making singularly boring what is in fact a defining and terrible experience.

And so as I waded through account after account of queer domestic abuse, little details stood out. This is the one that stuck with me the most:

A woman named Anne Franklin wrote an essay about her own abuse in *Gay Community News* in 1984. Her blonde, femme lover—a healer who gave massages and did star charts; who had, before meeting her, almost become a nun—once stoned her on a beach in France. "I know it sounds incredible," she wrote. "The image is cartoonish." She swam out into the water to escape the stoning. (The *stoning*.[52] This image has followed me for so long; what both has been and is a punishment for homosexuality, inflicted by the woman she loved. Swimming out into the ocean to get away. *Stone*. Stone butch. Stonewall. Queer history studded with stones, like jewelry.) "Later," she wrote, "we both laughed about it." Laughed about how she, Anne, was stoned on a beach in France. How she ran deeper and deeper into the water, like D-Day in reverse.

---

52. I think about this because it gets at this question of the way that queer abuse feels like—is—homophobia, the same way abuse in heterosexual relationships feels like—is—sexism. I am doing this because I can get away with it; I can get away with it because you exist on some cultural margin, some societal periphery.

## *Dream House as* Anechoic Chamber

During a visit to Iowa City, you go to an anechoic chamber deep in the earth. A friend comes with you, and as you are both led down the stairs it occurs to you that this is not unlike the opening of "The Cask of Amontillado." Your guide ushers you inside and swings the heavy door shut behind you, and the two of you lie on your backs on a metal dock that hangs in the air.

Here, and only here, everything makes a sound. The thrum and rush of your blood, your liquid swallows. Even your tongue running along the upper ridge of your mouth, which sounds like a piece of furniture being dragged over a bed of gravel. Here, your body is exactly as grotesque as you know it to be. Here, you are not dead, but everything around you might as well be.

There are no hallucinations, exactly, except for a strange buzzing on the edge of your hearing, like, your friend observes, cicadas at the height of summer. The buzzing isn't there, of course; your minds are simply imbuing the silence. You could go mad if you stay here too long, you think. Your mind would fill in the gaps and the blanks and God knows what it would fill them with.

What happens when there are no echoes, here in this underground crypt? You clap and clap but nothing answers back.

# *Dream House as* Generation Starship

Eventually, everyone forgets. That's the worst part, maybe. It's been so long since anyone's seen Earth; so long since that first crew made their way shipward, leaving behind their beloved planet wreathed in smoke and ice. They had to get out—they knew it, everyone knew it, but they were lucky, and found a ship.

And they set course to Somewhere Else and settled down, and when they had children they told their children the story of where they used to live. They left out the worst parts, maybe, because even now, surrounded by chrome and glass and stars, the acute bite of the planet's betrayal has lessened. And by the time they passed on, and the ship was still careening Away, the children of the children of the first crew had only the faintest wisps of understanding of what Used to Be. By the time they got to Somewhere Else (a beautiful planet, with singing stones and citrine trees and soil that smelled like cumin and water you could walk over), no one could even remember why they'd left Earth to begin with.

"I suppose it must have been terrible," they said uncertainly. "We took so much effort to leave. It must have been the worst place."

But that nagging sense of doubt was so profound they eventually gave it a name:

*Nonstalgia* (noun)
1.  The unsettling sensation that you are never be able to fully access the past; that once you are departed from an event, some essential quality of it is lost forever.
2.  A reminder to remember: just because the sharpness of the sadness has faded does not mean that it was not, once, terrible. It means only that time and space, creatures of infinite girth and tenderness, have stepped between the two of you, and they are keeping you safe as they were once unable to.

# *Dream House as* L'esprit de L'escalier

When I was preparing to fly to Cuba with my brother to see our ancestral home, I discovered that Santa Clara, Cuba—the city where my grandfather was born and raised, where he was once forced to eat a soup made from his pet rooster—is the sister city of Bloomington, Indiana. How was this possible? Of all the cities in the world, how were these two connected by such an arbitrary umbilical cord?

After we got there, we took an air-conditioned car from Havana to Varadero, then a hot, fragrant bus from Varadero to Santa Clara. I barely speak Spanish; my brother does and had also been there before, and he was sweet and supportive and vulnerable and took good care of me. As if my stomach sensed my stress, I got sick, very sick, and one morning spent four hours within twenty feet of my grandfather's childhood home vomiting so hard I strained my diaphragm in the watery dawn light. Afterward, the owner of the *casa particular* did a spell on me; performed some sort of obscure prayer with a measuring tape, banished my indigestion (as she called it) to somewhere else. "It's not me," she said. "I am merely a conduit to God, praise God." Then she made me drink an entire bottle of tonic water, which I'd never had without gin.

Walking around Santa Clara was beautiful and eerie, because I couldn't stop thinking about my grandfather walking through these streets. I also kept imagining that we were walking around a parallel map in Bloomington, Indiana. That's how sister cities *should* work: I could walk around both at the same time, separated by some thin, mystical scrim, and if I went to the right place at the right time I could peek into the other one. I could twitch a curtain next to a certain chicken and be staring at the Dream House, at the people who live there now.

The streets were filled with people and taxis drawn by bikes and horses and midcentury cars in varying states of disrepair. The famous hotel on the square was the same color scheme as my grandparents' former house in Maryland.

We approached a school, where children in uniform were pouring out of the entrance. "That's where Granddaddy went to school," my brother said. "Right there." He swung his finger to a nearby bank on the same square. "When I was here with Granddaddy," he said, "he told me a story about how one day he was heading home from school when he got caught in a downpour, so he went under the roof of the bank to stay dry until it stopped. An expensive car pulled up and the window rolled down. It was a rich, white Cuban man. He summoned Granddaddy to the window."

"What did he want?"

"I don't know. But he probably thought, 'Oh, I can summon this little brown kid out into the rain to do, I know, whatever, and he'll do it.' But Granddaddy refused, and the man kept gesturing, and eventually Granddaddy told him to go fuck himself."

This was how my brother told the story. I can't exactly imagine my grandfather—a funny, affable man who left Santa Clara and Cuba altogether, and loved Radio Shack and free pens and watches and tinkering with electronics and building birdhouses, who at that moment was back in the United States slipping down the embankment of dementia—telling anyone to go fuck himself, and yet I recognize this version of my grandfather all the same. He didn't apologize, or sob, or beg.

My brother and I drank watery El Presidentes at a café near the bank underneath a tapestry of Che, and I let the phrase *go fuck yourself* roll around in my mouth; a satisfying response, years too late.

# *Dream House as* Vaccine

When I was a kid, I learned that you develop immunity when an illness rages through your body. Your body is brilliant, even when you are not. It doesn't just heal—it learns. It remembers. (All of this, of course, if the virus doesn't kill you first.)

After the Dream House, I developed a sixth sense. It goes off at random times—meeting a new classmate or coworker, a friend's new girlfriend, a stranger at a party. A physical revulsion that comes on the heels of nothing at all, something akin to the sour liquid rush of saliva that precedes vomiting. Inconvenient, irritating, but important: my brilliant body's brilliant warning.

# *Dream House as* Ending

That there's a real ending to anything is, I'm pretty sure, the lie of all auto-biographical writing. You have to choose to stop somewhere. You have to let the reader go.

Where to stop this story? Val's and my wedding, on a hot day in June? Some narratively satisfying confrontation between the woman from the Dream House and me? If you grasp the story by the base and pull, will the ripping sound indicate the looseness of the roots? What is left behind in the soil?

Should I loop back to a memory from the Dream House? A lovely one? Will that work, a contrast between what could have been and what was? A memory of the two of us freshly returned from a local winery, sipping on a spicy Zinfandel and eating some kind of feta dip and telling a story?

One day the woman from the Dream House will die, and I will die, and Val will die, and John and Laura will die, and my brother will die, and my parents will die, and her parents will die, and everyone who ever knew any of us will die. Is that the end of the story? Time's mindless, chattering advancement?

There is a Panamanian folktale that ends with: "My tale goes only to here; it ends, and the wind carries it off." It's the only true kind of ending.

Sometimes you have to tell a story, and somewhere, you have to stop.

# *Dream House as* Epilogue

I wrote a large part of this book in rural eastern Oregon.[53] I stayed in a cabin at the edge of a playa, a lake that had mostly dried up during the summer. That part of the world is high desert country; the weather was cold at night and hot during the day. The air was so bone-dry I drank water every hour but still felt unquenchably thirsty. One morning a drop of blood plopped wetly onto my desk, and I went to the bathroom and used toilet paper to stanch the nosebleed. When I walked back I realized I'd left a *pat–pat–pat* trail of blood across the floor.

All day I sat and watched dust devils kick up at the far edge of the once-lake.[54] I was told there was still a bit of water out there, but it would take four miles of walking to reach it. It was like an alien landscape; it made me think of the salt flats of Utah or old episodes of *Star Trek*. I hiked to some caves where eagles roosted and the earth below their nests was littered with a mulch of fur and bone. An owl left half a rabbit on my doorstep; in the morning, something else had dragged it away and left a streak of gore.

After dinner I went out on the playa with the other residents. First we waded through a soft, undulating field of dry grasses that reached our shoulders. Then there was a rim of soil fine as confectioner's sugar; it felt as if we were tromping through moondust. Then the soil solidified and broke into thousands, millions of pieces, beautiful, geometric patterns. As we continued to walk, the earth began to crunch in a satisfying way beneath our feet. When we had hiked out far enough, the soil got looser and softer, like the cushy rubber mulch underneath a jungle gym. After a while, the smell changed: it was a little like sulfur and a little like bleach, the scent of a linden tree, the unmistakable scent of—as I said to the other residents,

---

53. Thompson, *Motif-Index of Folk-Literature*, Type D2161.3.6.1, Magic restoration of cut-out tongue.
54. Thompson, *Motif-Index of Folk-Literature*, Types A920.1.5, Bodies of water from tears; A133.1, Giant god drinks lakes dry.

regretting it even as the word was slipping from my mouth—semen. No one else agreed with me, or if they did, they didn't admit it. I reached down and picked up a chunk of dried earth and the soil underneath was damp: the memory of the lake.

A forest fire broke out on a minor mountain near our horizon. I drove past it one afternoon, watched as impossibly orange flames licked their way up the incline, leaving behind glossy, burnt sage and sticks of trees and still-flaming fence posts and, inexplicably, patches of unburnt space, where chance let something live. A helicopter dipped around like a dragonfly and dropped shimmering sheets of water down to the earth.

I went into town to sit in the library's air-conditioning. The librarian wanted to talk to me about the fire. She told me that forest fires are a danger to bulls and cows, but not deer. "They never find deer carcasses after these things," she said. "Deer know how to get out of the way. But bulls and cows, you can't get them to move for anything. Fire comes, and they just don't know what to do with themselves."

On the way back, the toxic amber smoke floated over the sun. That night, it was still burning. I walked out onto my porch to watch, and even as mosquitoes descended to feast I couldn't look away from the sight: a nearly full moon illuminating fast-moving clouds, and the distant, golden pulse of fire over the mountain, glowing like a second sunrise.

The next morning, while I was writing, something emerged from the grass mere feet from my window: a young buck with velvety antlers and comically long and expressive ears. He did not seem to notice me and settled down comfortably in the shade of a tree. I was utterly transfixed by him, a stray remnant of my childhood love of horses. I left him some baby carrots, hoping to let him know I meant no harm, but he didn't eat them, and within a few hours the air desiccated them into white, withered sticks.

Every time I moved, he turned and watched me with black eyes. When he stopped noticing me—when I'd been sitting reading or writing for a while—he relaxed as much as a deer can relax. His eyes blinked more languidly. He nibbled greenery, chased flies away, whisked his ears and tail through the air. I even once saw him lick his lips, and then yawn. The intimacy, the trust, would have been almost unbearable, if I thought it was trust.

Once I walked by the window and there were two of them, two bucks, sitting under the tree. Their fur looked soft, and they panted in the heat like large, beautiful dogs. But my foot creaked on the floorboards, and they bounded liquidly away through the grass. Half a mile away, they were still running.

A few days later, the full moon rose—blood-red because of the smoke—and I went for a hike on the lake. As the moon climbed higher and higher, it escaped the smoke and became a bright coin against the sky. Every detail of the cracked soil was surreally crisp; the crevices dark and deep. I wished everything had this much clarity. I wished I had always lived in this body, and you could have lived here with me, and I could have told you it's all right, it's going to be all right.

When I turned around, my dark silver moon-shadow walked in front of me as I made my way back to the shore.

My tale goes only to here; it ends, and the wind carries it to you.

# Afterword

In an essay about Joanna Russ's *How to Suppress Women's Writing*, Lee Mandelo calls women's literary history "written on sand." I can't think of a more apt metaphor for the process of writing this book, which relied on finding texts that talked about queer people and domestic abuse; two topics that have, historically, been hidden away, or rarely talked about. At times it didn't feel like I was writing at all; it felt like I was pinning down fragments of history with well-aimed throws of a knife before they could shift or melt away.

A note about language: Throughout this book, I have made a series of linguistic and rhetorical choices regarding labels and identifying terminology. Here, I primarily use *lesbian* and *queer woman*, and I do not explicitly talk about gay or queer men, or gender-nonconforming people, though they too experience domestic abuse. I made these choices for a few reasons. First, I am a more-or-less cisgendered queer woman and feel most comfortable writing through that specific lens. Second, much of the historical source material I found and drew from was primarily focused on cisgender lesbians and their communities. Third, while it is cumbersome to make every instance on the page include every potential identifier, what is even more unthinkable is suggesting that the histories, experiences, and struggles of all queer people are somehow interchangeable, when they absolutely are not. If there are failures within these pages, they are mine and mine alone.

*In the Dream House* is by no means meant to be a comprehensive account of contemporary research about same-sex domestic abuse or its history. That book, as far as I can tell, has yet to be written. One day—when it is written, if it is written—I hope this very rough, working attempt at a canon will be useful as a resource, in addition to honoring the work that has gone before.

There isn't a lot of writing about queer domestic abuse and sexual assault. But what I did find, kept me going. I read Conner Habib's heart-stopping essay "If You Ever Did Write Anything about Me, I'd Want It to Be about Love" in the immediate aftermath of my abuse, and it devastated me and also gave me something to hold on to. A few years later, Jane Eaton Hamilton's exquisite "Never Say I Didn't Bring You Flowers" gave me new ways to think about what had happened to me. When I was trying to finish this memoir, Leah Horlick's lush and devastating poetry collection *For Your Own Good* slayed me with its beauty. Melissa Febos's essay "Abandon Me" traced queer relationship trauma with brilliance and candor. A chapter in Sawyer Lovett's *Retrospect: A Tazewell's Favorite Eccentric Zine Anthology*—"Hello . . ."—came to me just when I needed it. Terry Castle's *The Professor* made me laugh out loud more than once, which was a pretty shocking thing to do in the middle of writing this book.

Other useful books and resources included *Naming the Violence: Speaking Out About Lesbian Battering*, edited by Kerry Lobel (Seal Press, 1986); "Building a Second Closet: Third Party Responses to Victims of Lesbian Partner Abuse," by Claire M. Renzetti (*Family Relations*, 1989); "Lavender Bruises: Intra-Lesbian Violence, Law and Lesbian Legal Theory," by Ruthann Robson (*Golden Gate University Law Review*, 1990); "Prosecutorial Activism: Confronting Heterosexism in a Lesbian Battering Case," by Angela West (*Harvard Women's Law Journal*, 1992); *Boots of Leather, Slippers of Gold: The History of a Lesbian Community*, by Elizabeth Lapovsky Kennedy and Madeline Davis (Routledge, 1993); *Lesbian Choices*, by Claudia Card (Columbia University Press, 1995): "Describing without Circumscribing: Questioning the Construction of Gender in the Discourse of Intimate Violence," by Phyllis Goldfarb (*Boston College Law School*, 1996); "Toward a Black Lesbian Jurisprudence," by Theresa Raffaele Jefferson (*Boston College Third World Law Journal*, 1998); *Same-Sex Domestic Violence: Strategies for Change*, edited by Beth Leventhal and Sandra E. Lundy (Sage Publications, 1999); *Taking Back Our Lives: A Call to Action for the Feminist Movement*, by Ann Russo (Routledge, 2001); *Sapphic Slashers: Sex, Violence, and American Modernity*, by Lisa Duggan (Duke University Press, 2001); *No More Secrets: Violence in Lesbian Relationships*, by Janice L. Ristock (Routledge, 2002); "The Closet Becomes Darker for the Abused: A Perspective on Lesbian Partner Abuse," by Marnie J. Franklin (*Cardozo Women's Law Journal*, 2003); "Constructing the Battered Woman," by Michelle VanNatta (*Feminist Studies*, 2005); and "When Is a Battered Woman Not a Battered Woman? When She Fights Back," by Leigh Goodmark (*Yale Journal of Law & Feminism*, 2008). I was also lucky to be able to access an incredible wealth of gay and lesbian and feminist periodicals with decades of writing on this subject, including *Sinister Wisdom*, *Gay Community News*, *Off Our Backs*, *Lesbian Connection*, *Matrix*, and the *Network News: The Newsletter of the Network for Battered Lesbians*.

To all of these writers, academics, archives, publications, and presses: thank you for your activism, your scholarship, and your wisdom.

# Acknowledgments

This book would have been impossible without the resources and support of the University of Pennsylvania, the Lesbian Herstory Archives, the Special Collections and University Archives at the University of Oregon, Yaddo, Playa, the Wurlitzer Foundation, and Bard College. Many thanks to Tracy Fontil, for her impeccable and thorough research, and the Bassini Foundation for sponsoring her apprenticeship.

Thank you to Dorothy Allison for her wisdom; Elliott Battzekek and Sawyer Lovett at Big Blue Marble Bookstore for their insight; Jane Marie at the *Hairpin* for publishing my first writing on this subject; Jen Wang and Jess Row for their musical expertise; Kendra Albert for leading me to resources on archival silence; Kevin Brockmeier for reading and being encouraging about an early draft of this memoir; David Korzenik for his legal advice; Mark Mayer for his sharp line edits and tender encouragement; Michelle Huneven for her thoughtful edits on "A Girl's Guide to Sexual Purity" when it was published in the *Los Angeles Review of Books*; Nikki Gloudeman for editing "Gaslight" for *Medium* and Matt Higginson for commissioning it; Sam Chang for her all-around excellence and also for directing me to Terry Castle's *The Professor*; Sofia Samatar for our many conversations about the radical possibilities of nonfiction; Ted Chiang for teaching me about time travel; Yuka Igarashi at *Catapult* for editing and publishing "The Moon Over the River Lethe"; and the vultures who sat in a tree over my head as I finished this book, for clearing away the rot.

I am, as always, in debt to my editors Ethan Nosowsky and Yana Makuwa (this book is infinitely better for their insight); my brilliant and scarily capable agent, Kent Wolf; and the entire team at Graywolf, for their tireless efforts, boundless faith, and endless good cheer.

I am deeply grateful to Amy, Ben, Bennett, Carleen, E.J., Evan, John, Laura, Rebecca, Rebekah, and Tony for their love, friendship, and stabilizing presence during those days; Chris, Emma, Julia, Karen, Lara, and Sam for listening when my pain was fresh and inarticulate; Audrey, R.K., and all the other members of the weirdest, gayest First Wives' Club ever, for trusting me with their stories; and Margaret, for putting the pieces together.

And of course, the biggest thanks go to my wife, Val—my plot twist, my fate, my fairy-tale ending—who challenges me and comforts me and allows me to splash details of our lives all over the place. I'd do it all again, baby. It brought me you.

CARMEN MARIA MACHADO's debut short story collection, *Her Body and Other Parties*, was a finalist for the National Book Award, the Kirkus Prize, LA Times Book Prize Art Seidenbaum Award for First Fiction, the Dylan Thomas Prize, and the PEN/Robert W. Bingham Prize for Debut Fiction, and the winner of the Bard Fiction Prize, the Lambda Literary Award for Lesbian Fiction, the Shirley Jackson Award, and the National Book Critics Circle's John Leonard Prize. In 2018, the *New York Times* listed *Her Body and Other Parties* as a member of "The New Vanguard," one of "15 remarkable books by women that are shaping the way we read and write fiction in the 21st century."

Her essays, fiction, and criticism have appeared in the *New Yorker*, the *New York Times*, *Granta*, *Tin House*, *VQR*, *McSweeney's Quarterly Concern*, the *Believer*, *Guernica*, *Best American Science Fiction & Fantasy*, *Best American Nonrequired Reading*, and elsewhere. She holds an MFA from the Iowa Writers' Workshop and has been awarded fellowships and residencies from the Guggenheim Foundation, the Michener-Copernicus Foundation, the Elizabeth George Foundation, the CINTAS Foundation, Yaddo, Hedgebrook, and the Millay Colony for the Arts. She is the writer in residence at the University of Pennsylvania and lives in Philadelphia with her wife.

The text of *In the Dream House* is set in Adobe Caslon Pro.

Book design by Rachel Holscher.

Composition by Bookmobile Design and Digital Publisher Services,
Minneapolis, Minnesota.

Manufactured by Friesens on acid-free, 100 percent postconsumer wastepaper.